Q U A R T E T   E N C O U N T E R S

THE PSYCHOANALYSIS OF FIRE

The subject of this unusual book is best described by the author. 'We are going to study a problem that no one has managed to approach objectively, one in which the initial charm of the object is so strong that it still has the power to warp the minds of the clearest thinkers and to keep bringing them back to the poetic fold in which dreams replace thought and poems conceal theorems. This problem is the psychological problem posed by our convictions about fire. It seems to me so definitely psychological in nature that I do not hesitate to speak of a psychoanalysis of fire.'

GASTON BACHELARD

Gaston Bachelard (1884–1962) was a philosopher whose training in the sciences gave him a unique profile in the world of literary criticism to which he turned. An admirer of Husserl and Jung, he was one of the most original and stimulating thinkers of the twentieth century.

GASTON BACHELARD

The Psychoanalysis of Fire

Translated from the French by
ALAN C.M. ROSS
With an Introduction by
NORTHROP FRYE

QUARTET ENCOUNTERS

Quartet Books London New York

Published in Great Britain by Quartet Books Limited 1987
A member of the Namara Group
27/29 Goodge Street, London W1P 1FD

First published by Beacon Press in 1964

Published in the United Kingdom by Quartet Books
by arrangement with Beacon Press 1987

British Library Cataloguing in Publication Data

Bachelard, Gaston
The psychoanalysis of fire.
1. Psychoanalysis
I. Title II. La psychanalyse du feu.
English
150.19'5 BF173

ISBN 0-7043-0022-2

Reproduced, printed and bound in Great Britain
by The Camelot Press plc, Southampton

Contents

Introduction by Northrop Frye

Literary critics have been aware of the great importance of Bachelard's work for many years, but this is the first time *The Psychoanalysis of Fire* has been available in English. Professor Ross's lucid and eloquent translation gives an excellent sense of the original, which has a subversive wit reminding the English reader of the prose style of the nineteenth-century Samuel Butler. I speak of literary critics, because, as its conclusion makes clear, this is the area in which *The Psychoanalysis of Fire* lies, despite its title and the numerous references to its author's earlier scientific works. Nearly a century ago Thomas Huxley, discussing the limitations of the scientific method, remarked: "I cannot conceive how the phenomena of consciousness, as such, are to be brought within the bounds of physical science." He did not mean that no science of psychology would ever be possible, but that the process of perception could not nullify itself, so to speak, by becoming objective to itself. Sciences are placed at various angles to the perceiving process, as physics is at an angle to the primitive categories of hot, cold, moist and dry, or to the primitive perception of red and blue. Psychology occupies another angle of perception, and Bachelard has begun to isolate still another, a basis for a systematic development of the critical study of the arts.

The scientific procedure normally begins empirically, with reality thought of first of all as "out there," after which it gradually becomes incorporated into an intellectual construct. The arts, on the other hand, begin with a constructing power, generally called imagination, and embody it in forms with a clarity of communication that makes them objects of perception to others. The units of this constructing power are analogy and identity, which appear in literature as the figures of simile and metaphor. To the imagination, fire is not a separable datum of experience: it is already linked by analogy and identity with a dozen other aspects of experience. Its heat is analogous to the internal heat we feel as warm-blooded animals; its sparks are analogous to seeds, the units of life; its flickering movement is analogous to vitality; its flames are phallic symbols, providing a further analogy to the sexual act, as the ambiguity of the word "consummation" indicates; its transforming power is analogous to purgation. These links of analogy are so adhesive that they spread all over the universe: we see in this book, as often elsewhere, how the pursuit of one mythical complex tends to absorb all other myths into it. The reader should consult Bachelard's books on the other three elements for a corrective.

It is possible to take up a construct based on such analogies and correspondences, and then apply it to the external world as a key to the explanation of its phenomena. The typical examples of such constructs are in occultism, though they exist also in the Ptolemaic cosmology of the Middle Ages, with its correspondences of the seven metals, seven planets, seven days of the week, and the like. From one point of view, a somewhat narrow one, such constructs are both bastard art and bastard science, combining the limitations of the two with the genuine achievements of neither. A more liberal view might see them rather as helping to expand the horizons of both. We notice that poetry shows a strong affinity for constructs based on analogy and symmetry, Ptolemaic in Dante, occult in the Romantics and their successors down to Yeats. For the poet, the elements will always be earth, air, fire and water; for the poet, the sun will always rise and set as it moves around the earth. It is only in science where such myths are a nuisance; yet even in science the tendency to make them is extraordinarily persistent. Almost every major group of discoveries in science brings with it a great wave of speculative cosmologies based on analogies to them. Bachelard gives many quaint examples from eighteenth-century science, along with such analogy-myths as "spontaneous combustion." He could have gone on with the nineteenth-century speculations about "odic force" and the vitalist philosophies that followed early Darwinism, both of them pure fire-myths.

The proper place for all such analogy-making is literature, or, in earlier times, the mythology which eventually develops into literature. Bachelard does not explicitly say that mythology, considered as a body of stories, is potential literature, but the whole trend of his book is towards that principle. He quotes some of the myths about the origin of fire which include the theme of a woman's hiding fire in her belly. This feat is known to be anatomically impossible by those who are telling and listening to the story, so why should it be told? We recall that many similar stories are told about water, that there are more highly developed stories of the Jonah type; where a human being disappears into a monstrous belly, that the conception of a hidden interior world of fire is the basis of Dante's Inferno—in short, the story illustrates a structural principle of story-telling, and its study eventually falls into the area of literary criticism.

Centuries ago it was believed that the four possible combinations of the four "principles," hot, cold, moist and dry, produced, in the organic world, the four humors, and, in the inorganic world, the four elements. The hot and dry combination produced choler and fire, the hot and moist blood and air, the cold and moist phlegm and water, the cold and dry melancholy and earth. The four elements are not a conception of much use to modern chemistry—that is, they are not the elements of nature. But, as Bachelard's book and its companion works show, and as an abundance of literature down to Eliot's *Quartets* also shows, earth, air, water and fire are still the four elements of imaginative experience, and always will be. Similarly, the four humors are not a conception of any use to modern medicine; they are not the constituents of human temperament. But they may be the elements of imaginative perception, and Bachelard's analysis of Hoffmann's fire-images is linked to a suggestion that poets may be "humors" not in their bodies or characters but in their poetry, a poetic temperament being reflected in a preference for the corresponding element.

What Bachelard calls a "complex" might better be called something else, to avoid confusion with the purely psychological complexes of actual life. I should call it a myth, because to me a myth is a structural principle in literature. For example, there is, in Bachelard's sense, a literary Oedipus complex: it appears in every comedy in which the hero is a son outwitting his father to get possession of a courtesan or other tabooed female. It is undoubtedly related to the Oedipus complex discussed by Freud, but can hardly be treated as identical with it. The "complexes" dealt with in this book are actually the points at which literary myth becomes focussed on its cardinal points of creation, redemption and apocalypse.

In the earlier part of our cultural tradition the fire-world was most significantly the world of heavenly bodies between heaven proper and the earth. The Spirit descends from above in tongues of fire; the seraphim are angels of fire; the gods who preceded the angels are in charge of the planets; for Christianity the world of superior spirits is all that is left of the unfallen world that God originally planned. The fire-world as the unfallen world of pre-creation appears in Bachelard as the "Novalis complex." The return of man to his original home, the complementary myth of ascending fire, is symbolized by the funeral pyre of Hercules (in the fourth section of Eliot's "Little Gidding," for example, this image is brought into direct contrast with the image of fire descending from the Holy Spirit), and comes into all the imagery of purgatorial fire in Dante and elsewhere. With the Romantics this more specifically human fire, which symbolizes the raising of the human state to a quasi-divine destiny, becomes more purely a "Prometheus complex," especially to the more revolutionary Romantics, Shelley, Byron, Victor Hugo, who feel, like Ahab in *Moby Dick*, that the right form of fire-worship is defiance. The Last Judgment, the destruction of the world by fire and the absorption of the human soul into the soul of fire, is the "Empedocles complex."

Thus the myth of "spontaneous combustion" is used by Dickens in *Bleak House*, to describe the death of Krook. In his preface Dickens stubbornly defends the actuality of the conception, and refers to some of the authorities quoted by Bachelard, including Le Cat. When Dickens finally says: "I shall not abandon the facts until there shall have been a considerable Spontaneous Combustion of the testimony on which human occurrences are usually received"—in other words the Last Judgment—we begin to get a clue to the real reason why Dickens felt that such a device was essential to his story. This is merely one example of the kind of expanding insight into literature which can take off from Bachelard's witty and pungent study.

NORTHROP FRYE

The Psychoanalysis of Fire

Introduction

I must not look on
reality as being like
myself.

PAUL ELUARD

We have only to speak of an object to think that we are being objective. But, because we chose it in the first place, the object reveals more about us than we do about it. What we consider to be our fundamental ideas concerning the world are often indications of the immaturity of our minds. Sometimes we stand in wonder before a chosen object; we build up hypotheses and reveries; in this way we form convictions which have all the appearance of true knowledge. But the initial source is impure: the first impression is not a fundamental truth. In point of fact, scientific objectivity is possible only if one has broken first with the immediate object, if one has refused to yield to the seduction of the initial choice, if one has checked and contradicted the thoughts which arise from one's first observation. Any objective examination, when duly verified, refutes the results of the first contact with the object. To start with, everything must be called into question: sensation, common sense, usage however constant, even etymology, for words, which are made for singing and enchanting, rarely make contact with thought. Far from marvelling at the object, objective thought must treat it ironically. Without this malign vigilance we would never adopt a truly objective attitude. When we are dealing with men, our equals and our brothers, our method should be based on sympathy. But when confronted with this inert world whose life is not ours, which suffers none of our sorrows nor is exalted by any of our joys, we must restrain all our enthusiasms, we must repress our personal feelings. The axes of poetry and of science are opposed to one another from the outset. All that philosophy can hope to accomplish is to make poetry and science complementary, to unite them as two well-defined opposites. We must oppose, then, to the enthusiastic, poetic mind the taciturn, scientific mind, and for the scientific mind an attitude of preliminary antipathy is a healthy precaution.

We are going to study a problem that no one has managed to approach objectively, one in which the initial charm of the object is so strong that it still has the power to warp the minds of the clearest thinkers and to keep bringing them back to the poetic fold in which dreams replace thought and poems conceal theorems. This problem is the psychological problem posed by our convictions about fire. It seems to me so definitely psychological in nature that I do not hesitate to speak of a psychoanalysis of fire.

Contemporary science has almost completely neglected the truly primordial problem that the phenomena of fire pose for the untutored mind. In the course of time the chapters on fire in chemistry textbooks have become shorter and shorter. There are, indeed, a good many modern books on chemistry in which it is impossible to find any mention of flame or fire. *Fire is no longer a reality for science.* Fire, that striking immediate object, that object which imposes itself as a first choice ahead of many other phenomena, no longer offers any perspective for scientific investigation. It seems, then, that it would be instructive from a psychological point of view to trace the way in which this phenomenological value has become inflated and to study how a problem which had been a prime concern of scientific research for centuries was suddenly broken down into smaller problems or set aside without ever having been solved. When, as I have done on many occasions, one asks educated persons and even eminent scientists, "What is fire?", one receives vague or tautological answers which unconsciously repeat the most ancient and fanciful philosophical theories. The reason for this is that the question has fallen within a zone that is only partially objective, a zone in which personal intuitions and scientific experiments are intermingled. As a matter of fact, we shall demonstrate that our intuitions of fire—more perhaps than of any other phenomenon—are heavily charged with fallacies from the past. These intuitions lead us to form immediate convictions about a problem which really should be solved by strict measurement and experimentation.

In one of my early books[1] I attempted to describe, in connection with heat phenomena, a clearly-defined axis of scientific objectivization. Here I showed how geometry and algebra gradually contributed their abstract forms and principles so that experimentation might be canalized into a scientific path. It is now the other axis—no longer the axis of objectivization but that of subjectivity—that I would like to explore in order to illustrate the double perspectives that might be attached to all problems connected with the knowledge of any particular reality, even a well-defined reality. If we were correct in our theorizing about the real implication of subject and object then we should attempt to make a clearer distinction between the pensive man and the thinker, without, however, any real hope of ever being able to make an absolute distinction between them. In any case it is the pensive man whom we wish to study here, the man pensively seated by his fireplace in complete solitude at a time when the fire is burning brightly as if it were the very voice of this solitude. We shall have, then, many opportunities to show the dangers that first impressions, sympathetic attractions, and careless reveries hold for true scientific knowledge. We shall easily be able to observe the observer and so arrive at the principles underlying this value-laden or rather this hypnotized form of observation that is involved in gazing into a fire. Finally, this slightly hypnotized condition, that is surprisingly constant in all fire watchers, is highly conducive to psychoanalytical investigation. A winter's evening with the wind howling around the house and a bright fire within is all that is required to make the grieving soul give voice to its memories and sorrows:

> It is the muted voice of the dying winter embers
> Which enchants this heart of mine,
> This heart which like the covered flame
> Sings as it is consumed.
>
> Toulet

But although this book is easy to write when we go about it line upon line, it seems to be quite impossible to give it a well-organized structure. To draw up a plan of human errors is an enterprise impossible of fulfillment. It is particularly difficult in the case of a task like ours, which cannot be treated on the historical plan because the conditions that led to reverie in the past have not been eliminated by contemporary scientific education. Even the scientist, when not practising his specialty, returns to the primitive scale of values. Thus it would be a vain undertaking to trace the historical development of a thought which has always run counter to the teachings of the history of science. Instead we shall devote part of our efforts to showing that reverie takes up the same primitive themes time and again and always operates as it would in primitive minds, and this in spite of the successes of systematic thought and even in face of the findings of scientific experiments.

Nor shall we situate our studies in a remote period in which it would be only too easy to illustrate the prevalence of fire worship. What appears, however, to be a worthwhile project is to establish the secret persistence of this idolatry of fire. Therefore the closer that the document we are using is to our own time the more forcefully will it demonstrate our thesis. Our aim will be to track down in historical records the permanent document that indicates a resistance to psychological evolution, that reveals the old man in the young child, the young child in the old man, the alchemist in the engineer. But since, for us, the past represents ignorance just as reverie represents futility, our aim will be as follows: to cure the mind of its happy illusions, to free it from the narcissism caused by the first contact with the object, to give it assurances other than mere possession, and powers of conviction other than mere warmth and enthusiasm, in short, to give the mind proofs that are not as unsubstantial as flames!

But we have already said enough to bring home to the reader the meaning of a *psychoanalysis* of the subjective convictions related to the knowledge of fire phenomena, or more briefly, of a psychoanalysis of fire. It will be by specific arguments that we shall make clear our general theses.

We would like, however, to add a further remark by way of warning. When our reader has finished reading this book he will in no way have increased his knowledge. This will not be entirely our fault, perhaps, but rather will be the price that must be paid for the method we have selected. When we turn inwards upon ourselves we turn aside from truth. When we carry out *inner* experiments, we inevitably contradict objective experiment. Again it must be repeated that in this book when we talk of our personal experiences we are demonstrating human errors. Our work is offered, then, as an example of that special psychoanalysis that we believe would form a useful basis for all objective studies. It is an illustration of the general theses put forward in our recent book, *The Formation of the Scientific Mind* (*La Formation de l'esprit scientifique*). The pedagogy of scientific instruction would be improved if we could demonstrate clearly how the fascination exerted by the object *distorts inductions*. It would not be difficult to write about water, air, earth, salt, wine and blood in the same way that we have dealt with fire in this brief outline. To tell the truth, these substances which receive an immediate emotional value and lead objective research to the study of non-general themes are less clearly double—less clearly subjective and objective—than fire; but nevertheless they too bear a false stamp, the false weight of unquestioned values. It would be more difficult but also more fruitful to use psychoanalysis to examine the bases for certain other more rational, less immediate and hence less affective concepts than those attached to our experiences of substances. If we succeeded in inspiring any imitators, we should urge them to study, from the same point of view as a psychoanalysis of objective knowledge, the notions of totality, of system, of element, evolution and development . . . One would have no trouble in discovering that underlying such notions is a system of heterogeneous values, indirect but of an undeniably affective nature. In all these examples one would find beneath the theories, more or less readily accepted by scientists and philosophers, convictions that are often quite ingenuous. These unquestioned convictions are so many extraneous flashes that bedevil the proper illumination that the mind must build up in any project of the discursive reason. Everyone should seek to destroy within himself these blindly accepted convictions. Everyone must learn to escape from the rigidity of the mental habits formed by contact with familiar experiences. Everyone must destroy even more carefully than his phobias, his "philias," his complacent acceptance of first intuitions.

To sum up, while we do not seek to instruct the reader, we should feel rewarded for our efforts if we can persuade him to practice an exercise at which we are a master: to laugh at oneself. No progress is possible in the acquisition of objective knowledge without this self-critical irony. Finally, it should be noted that we have cited only a very small portion of the documents that we have compiled in the course of our endless readings in the old scientific books of the seventeenth and eighteenth centuries. As a result, this short work is a mere outline of the subject. If it had been solely a question of recording stupid observations, it would have been only too easy to have written a large volume.

CHAPTER ONE

Fire and Respect:

The Prometheus Complex

Fire and heat provide modes of explanation in the most varied domains, because they have been for us the occasion for unforgettable memories, for simple and decisive personal experiences. Fire is thus a privileged phenomenon which can explain anything. If all that changes slowly may be explained by life, all that changes quickly is explained by fire. Fire is the ultra-living element. It is intimate and it is universal. It lives in our heart. It lives in the sky. It rises from the depths of the substance and offers itself with the warmth of love. Or it can go back down into the substance and hide there, latent and pent-up, like hate and vengeance. Among all phenomena, it is really the only one to which there can be so definitely attributed the opposing values of good and evil. It shines in Paradise. It burns in Hell. It is gentleness and torture. It is cookery and it is apocalypse. It is a pleasure for the *good* child sitting prudently by the hearth; yet it punishes any disobedience when the child wishes to play too close to its flames. It is well-being and it is respect. It is a tutelary and a terrible divinity, both good and bad. It can contradict itself; thus it is one of the principles of universal explanation.

Were it not for these initial values it takes on, neither the tolerance of common opinion which accepts the most flagrant contradictions nor the enthusiasm which accumulates, without proof, the most laudatory epithets, would be understandable. For example, what affection and what nonsense there is in this page written by a doctor at the end of the eighteenth century:

> I mean by this fire not a violent, tumultuous, irritating and unnatural heat which burns instead of cooking the bodily humors just as it does the foods; but rather that gentle, moderate, aromatic fire which is accompanied by a certain humidity having an affinity with that of blood and which penetrates the heterogeneous humors as well as the nutritious juices, separates them, wears them down, polishes the roughness and bitterness of their several parts and finally brings them to such a degree of gentleness and refinement that they are now adapted to our nature.[1]

In this page there is not a single argument, not a single epithet, which can be granted an objective meaning. And yet how convincing it is! To me it seems to combine the persuasive power of the doctor and the insinuating power of the remedy. Just as fire is the most insinuating of medicaments, so in extolling its virtues the doctor is at his most persuasive. In any case I never reread this page—let him who can explain this invincible association—without remembering the grave and kindly doctor with the gold watch who used to come to my bedside when I was a child and who would calm my worried mother with one learned word. It would be a winter's morning in our poor home. The fire would be shining in the hearth. They would give me syrup of Tolu. I can remember how I would lick the spoon. Where are they, those days filled with the warm smell of balsam and the hot aromas of the medicines?

When I was sick my father would light a fire in my room. He would take great care in arranging the logs over the kindling chips and in slipping the handful of shavings between the andirons. To fail to light the fire would have been incredibly stupid. I could not imagine my father having any equal in the performance of this function, which he would never allow anyone else to carry out. Indeed, I do not think I lit a fire myself before I was eighteen years old. It was only when I lived alone that I became master of my own hearth. But I still take special pride in the *art of kindling* that I learned from my father. I think I would rather fail to teach a good philosophy lesson than fail to light my morning fire. Thus how keenly sympathetic I am when I read in the work of a favorite author [Ducarla], who is usually occupied with scientific research, this page which to me is almost a page of personal memories:[2]

I have often amused myself with this trick when I was out visiting or when I had company at home: the fire would die down; for a long time the others would poke at it knowingly through a thick cloud of smoke, but in vain. Finally they would resort to chips and coal which often did not arrive in time; after the logs had been turned over a good many times, I would succeed in getting hold of the fire tongs, a feat that requires patience, audacity and some luck. I would even call a halt to the festivities while I pretended to cast a spell, like the faith healers to whom the Faculty of Medicine turns over a patient whose life is despaired of; then all I would do would be to put a few half-burned logs facing one another, often without those present noticing that I had touched anything. I would sit back, apparently without having done anything at all; they would look at me as if to tell me to get busy, and yet the flame would come and lay hold of the pile of logs; then they would accuse me of having thrown some kind of flash powder on it, and, in the end, would usually acknowledge that I had made the most of the draught; they did not go so far as to inquire into the complete, the effluent and the radiant kinds of heat, or into pyrospheres, translative speeds, and calorific series.

And Ducarla goes on to display both his domestic talents and his ambitious theoretical system of knowledge in which the propagation of fire is described as a geometric progression which follows "calorific series." In spite of this mathematical intrusion, the first principle of the "objective" thought of Ducarla is very evident, and its psychoanalysis is immediate: let us put glowing ember against glowing ember and the flame will come to brighten our hearth.

Perhaps the reader here can discern an example of the method that we propose to follow in our psychoanalysis of objective knowledge. It is really a question of finding how unconscious values affect the very basis of empirical and scientific knowledge. We must then show the mutual light which objective and social knowledge constantly sheds on subjective and personal knowledge, and vice versa. We must show in the scientific experiment traces of the experience of the child. Thus we shall be justified in speaking of an *unconscious of the scientific mind*—of the heterogeneous nature of certain concepts, and we shall see converging, in our study of any particular phenomenon, convictions that have been formed in the most varied fields.

For one thing, perhaps it has not been sufficiently noted that fire is more a *social reality* than a *natural reality*. To see the justification for this remark there is no need to go into lengthy considerations of the role of fire in primitive societies nor to insist on the technical difficulties involved in keeping a fire burning; all that is necessary is to practice some positive psychology by examining the structure and the education of a civilized mind. In point of fact, respect for fire is a respect that has been taught; it is not a natural respect. The reflex which makes us pull back our finger from the flame of a candle does not play any conscious role in our knowledge about fire. One may even be astonished that it has been accorded so much importance in textbooks on elementary psychology, where it is offered as the eternal example of the intervention of a sort of reflective thinking within the reflex, of a conscious thought in the midst of the most violent sensation. *In reality the social prohibitions are the first.* The natural experience comes only in second place to furnish a material proof which is *unexpected* and hence too obscure to establish an item of objective knowledge. The burn, that is to say the natural inhibition, by confirming the social interdictions, thereby only gives all the more value to the paternal intelligence in the child's eyes. Thus there is at the base of the child's knowledge of fire an interaction of the natural and the social in which the social is almost always dominant. Perhaps this can be seen better if we compare the pin-prick and the burn. They both cause reflexes. Why then are *points* not the object of respect and fear in the same way as fire? It is precisely because the social prohibitions concerning points are much weaker than the prohibitions concerning fire.

This, then, is the true basis for the respect shown to flame: if the child brings his hand close to the fire his father raps him over the knuckles with a ruler. Fire, then, can strike without having to burn. Whether this fire be flame or heat, lamp or stove, the parents' vigilance is the same. Thus fire is initially the object of a *general prohibition;* hence this conclusion: the social interdiction is our first *general knowledge* of fire. What we first learn about fire is that we must not touch it. As the child grows up, the prohibitions become intellectual rather than physical; the blow of the ruler is replaced by the angry voice; the angry voice by the recital of the dangers of fire, by the legends concerning fire from heaven. Thus the natural phenomenon is rapidly mixed in with complex and confused items of social experience which leave little room for the acquiring of an unprejudiced knowledge.

Consequently, since the prohibitions are primarily social interdictions, the problem of obtaining a personal knowledge of fire is the problem of *clever disobedience.* The child wishes to do what his father does, but far away from his father's presence, and so like a little Prometheus he steals some matches. He then heads for the fields where, in the hollow of a little valley, he and his companions build a secret fireplace that will keep them warm on the days when they decide to play truant from school. The city child has little acquaintance with the joys of the fire flaming up between three stones; he has not tasted the fried sloe nor the snail that has been placed all slimy on the fiery embers. He may very well escape the *Prometheus complex* whose action I have often experienced. Only this complex enables us to understand the interest that is always aroused by the rather trite legend of the father of Fire. Moreover, one must not hasten to confuse this Prometheus complex with the Oedipus complex of classical psychoanalysis. Doubtless the sexual components of reveries about fire are particularly intense, and we shall attempt in a later chapter to demonstrate this fact. Perhaps, however, it is better to designate all the shades of unconscious convictions by different formulas, until we can see later how the various complexes are related. As it happens, one of the advantages of the psychoanalysis of objective knowledge that we are proposing to carry out seems to be that we are examining a zone that is less deep than that in which the primitive instincts function; and it is because this zone is intermediary that it has a determinative action on clear thought, on scientific thought. To know facts and to make things are needs that we can characterize in themselves without necessarily having to relate them to the will to power. There is in man a veritable *will to intellectuality*. We underestimate the need to understand when we place it, as pragmatism and Bergsonism have done, under the absolute dependence of the principle of utility. We propose, then, to place together under the name of the *Prometheus complex* all those tendencies which impel us *to know* as much as our fathers, more than our fathers, as much as our teachers, more than our teachers. Now it is by handling the object, it is by perfecting our objective knowledge, that we can best hope to prove decisively that we have attained the intellectual level that we have so admired in our parents and in our teachers. The acquiring of supremacy through the drive of more powerful instincts naturally will appeal to a much greater number of individuals, but minds of a rarer stamp also must be examined by the psychologist. If pure intellectuality is exceptional, it is nonetheless very characteristic of a specifically human evolution. The Prometheus complex is the Oedipus complex of the life of the intellect.

CHAPTER TWO

Fire and Reverie:

The Empedocles Complex

Modern psychiatry has made clear the psychology of the pyromaniac. It has shown the sexual nature of his tendencies. On the other hand it has brought to light the serious traumatism that a psyche can suffer from the spectacle of a roof or haystack that has been set on fire, from the sight of the great blaze of fire shining against the night sky and extending out over the broad expanse of the ploughed fields. Almost always a case of incendiarism in the country is the sign of the diseased mind of some shepherd. Like bearers of sinister torches, these men of low degree transmit from age to age the contagion of their lonely dreams. The sight of a fire will cause some man to become a pyromaniac almost as inevitably as a pyromaniac will some day start a fire. Fire smolders in a soul more surely than it does under ashes. The arsonist is the most dissembling of criminals. At the asylum of Saint-Ylie, the pyromanic with the most marked tendencies is a very obliging fellow. There is only one thing that he claims he does not know how to do, that is to light the stove. Like psychiatry, classical psychoanalysis has long studied dreams about fire. They are among the clearest, the most distinct, those for which the sexual interpretation is the most certain. Therefore we shall not touch upon this problem.

Since we are limiting ourselves to psychoanalyzing a psychic layer that is less deep, more intellectualized, we must replace the study of dreams by the study of reverie, and, more particularly, in this little book we must study the reverie before the fire. In our opinion, this reverie is entirely different from the dream by the very fact that it is always more or less centered upon one object. The dream proceeds on its way in linear fashion, forgetting its original path as it hastens along. The reverie works in a star pattern. It returns to its center to shoot out new beams. And, as it happens, the reverie in front of the fire, the gentle reverie that is conscious of its well-being, is the most naturally centered reverie. It may be counted among those which best hold fast to their object or, if one prefers, to their pretext. Hence this solidity and this homogeneity which give it such charm that no one can free himself from it. It is so well defined that it has become banal to say, "We love to see a log fire burning in the fireplace." In this case it is a question of the quiet, regular, controlled fire that is seen when the great log emits tiny flames as it burns. It is a phenomenon both monotonous and brilliant, a really total phenomenon: it speaks and soars, and it sings.

The fire confined to the fireplace was no doubt for man the first object of reverie, the symbol of repose, the invitation to repose. One can hardly conceive of a philosophy of repose that would not include a reverie before a flaming log fire. Thus, in our opinion, to be deprived of a reverie before a burning fire is to lose the first use and the truly human use of fire. To be sure, a fire warms us and gives us comfort. But one only becomes fully aware of this comforting sensation after quite a long period of contemplation of the flames; one only receives comfort from the fire when one leans his elbows on his knees and holds his head in his hands. This attitude comes from the distant past. The child by the fire assumes it naturally. Not for nothing is it the attitude of the Thinker. It leads to a very special kind of attention which has nothing in common with the attention involved in watching or observing. Very rarely is it utilized for any other kind of contemplation. When near the fire, one must be seated; one must rest without sleeping; one must engage in reverie on a specific object.

Of course the supporters of the theory of the utilitarian formation of the mind will not accept a theory so facile in its idealism, and they will point out to us the multiple uses of fire in order to ascertain the exact interest that we have in it: not only does fire give heat, but it also cooks meats. As if the complex hearth, the peasant's hearth, precluded reverie!

From the notched teeth of the chimney hook there hung the black cauldron. The three-legged cooking pot projected over the hot embers. Puffing up her cheeks to blow into the steel tube, my grandmother would rekindle the sleeping flames. Everything would be cooking at the same time: the potatoes for the pigs, the choice potatoes for the family. For me there would be a fresh egg cooking under the ashes. The intensity of a fire cannot be measured by the egg timer; the egg was done when a drop of water, often a drop of saliva, would evaporate on the shell. Recently I was very much surprised to read that Denis Papin used the same procedure as my grandmother in tending his cooking pot. Before getting my egg I was condemned to eat a soup of bread and butter boiled to a pulp. One day, being a hot-tempered and impetuous child, I threw whole spoonfuls of my soup into the teeth of the chimney hook saying, "Eat, chimney hook, eat!" But on days when I was on my good behavior, they would bring out the waffle iron. Rectangular in form, it would crush down the fire of thorns burning red as the spikes of sword lilies. And soon the *gaufre* or waffle would be pressed against my pinafore, warmer to the fingers than to the lips. Yes, then indeed I was eating fire, eating its gold, its odor and even its crackling while the burning gaufre was crunching under my teeth. And it is always like that, through a kind of extra pleasure—like dessert—that fire shows itself a friend of man. It does not confine itself to cooking; it makes things crisp and crunchy. It puts the golden crust on the griddle cake; it gives a material form to man's festivities. As far back in time as we can go, the gastronomic value has always been more highly prized than the nutritive value, and it is in joy and not in sorrow that man discovered his intellect. The conquest of the superfluous gives us a greater spiritual excitement than the conquest of the necessary. Man is a creation of desire, not a creation of need.

But the reverie by the fireside has axes that are more philosophical. Fire is for the man who is contemplating it an example of a sudden change or development and an example of a circumstantial development. Less monotonous and less abstract than flowing water, even more quick to grow and to change than the young bird we watch every day in its nest in the bushes, fire suggests the desire to change, to speed up the passage of time, to bring all of life to its conclusion, to its hereafter. In these circumstances the reverie becomes truly fascinating and dramatic; it magnifies human destiny; it links the small to the great, the hearth to the volcano, the life of a log to the life of a world. The fascinated individual hears *the call of the funeral pyre.* For him destruction is more than a change, it is a renewal.

This very special and yet very general kind of reverie leads to a true complex in which are united the love and the respect for fire, the instinct for living and the instinct for dying. To save time one could call it the *Empedocles complex.* One can see its development in a curious work of George Sand. It is one of her early works, saved from oblivion by Aurore Sand. Perhaps this *Dreamer's Story* (*Histoire du Rêveur*) was written before the first trip to Italy, before the first Volcano, after the marriage but before the first love affair. In any case it bears the mark of the Volcano, imagined rather than described. This is often the case in literature. For example, one will find an equally typical page in the work of Jean-Paul Richter, who dreams that the sun, son of Earth, has been shot up to heaven through a mountain's erupting crater. But since the reverie is more instructive for us than the dream, let us follow the account in George Sand.

In order to obtain the view of Sicily in the early morning light as it stands out fiery red against the glittering ocean, the traveller makes his way up the slopes of Mount Etna as night is falling. He stops to sleep in the Goat Grotto, but, since sleep will not come, he dreams before his fire of birch logs; he naturally remains

. . . with his elbows leaning on his knees and his eyes fixed on the glowing embers of his fire from which white and blue flames escape in a thousand varied forms and undulations. "Now there," he thought to himself, "is a reduced image of the action of the flame and the movement of the lava during the eruptions of Mount Etna. Why have I not been called upon to contemplate this admirable spectacle in all its horrors?"

How can one admire a spectacle that one has never seen? But, as if to give us a better indication of the true axis of his *magnifying reverie*, the author continues:

Why have I not the eyes of an ant in order to admire this burning birch log? With what transports of blind joy and of love's frenzy these swarms of little white moths come to hurl themselves into it! For them this is the volcano in all its majesty. This is the spectacle of an immense conflagration. This dazzling light intoxicates and exalts them as the sight of the whole forest on fire would do for me.

Love, death and fire are united at the same moment. Through its sacrifice in the heart of the flames, the mayfly gives us a lesson in eternity. This total death which leaves no trace is the guarantee that our whole person has departed for the beyond. To lose everything in order to gain everything. The lesson taught by the fire is clear: "After having gained all through skill, through love or through violence you must give up all, you must annihilate yourself." (D'Annunzio, *Contemplation de la Mort.*) As Giono points out in his *Les Vraies Richesses* such is at any rate the intellectual urge "in old races, as among the Indians of India, or among the Aztecs, among people whose religious philosophy and religious cruelty have rendered anaemic to the point of total desiccation so that the head has become merely a globe of pure intelligence." Only these intellectualized people, these individuals subjected to the instincts of an intellectual formation, continues Giono "can force the door of the furnace and enter into the mystery of the fire."

This is something that George Sand is going to make clear to us. As soon as the reverie becomes concentrated, the genie of the Volcano appears. He dances "on blue and red embers . . . using as his mount a snowflake carried along by the hurricane." He carries the dreamer away beyond the quadrangular monument whose founding is traditionally attributed to Empedocles. "Come, my king. Put on your crown of white flame and blue sulphur from which there comes forth a dazzling rain of diamonds and sapphires." And the Dreamer, ready for the sacrifice, replies: "Here I am! Envelop me in rivers of burning lava, clasp me in your arms of fire as a lover clasps his bride. I have donned the red mantle. I have adorned myself in your colors. Put on, too, your burning gown of purple. Cover your sides with its dazzling folds. Etna, come, Etna! Break open your gates of basalt, spew forth your pitch and sulphur. Vomit forth the stone, the metal and the fire! . . ." In the heart of the fire, death is no longer death. "Death could not exist in that ethereal region to which you are carrying me . . . My fragile body may be consumed by the fire, my soul must be united with those tenuous elements of which you are composed." "Very well!" said the Spirit, casting over the Dreamer part of his red mantle, "Say farewell to the life of men and follow me into the life of phantoms."

Thus a reverie by the fireside, when the flame twists the frail birch branches, is sufficient to evoke the volcano and the funeral pyre. The bit of straw which flies away with the smoke is sufficient to urge us forward to meet our destiny. What better proof is there that the contemplation of fire brings us back to the very origins of philosophic thought? If fire, which, after all, is quite an exceptional and rare phenomenon, was taken to be a constituent element of the Universe, is it not because it is an element of human thought, the prime element of reverie?

When one has recognized a psychological complex, it

seems that one has a better and more synthetic understanding of certain poetic works. In point of fact a poetic work can hardly be unified except by a complex. If the complex is lacking, the work, cut off from its roots, no longer communicates with the unconscious. It appears cold, artificial, false. On the other hand even an unfinished work such as the *Empedokles* of Hölderlin, which has appeared in various readings containing numerous repetitions, nevertheless retains a certain unity because of the mere fact that it has been grafted upon the Empedocles complex. While Hyperion chooses a life which is mingled more intimately with that of Nature, Empedocles chooses a death which fuses him into the pure element of the Volcano. As M. Pierre Bertaux has aptly pointed out, these two solutions are more alike than it appears at first sight. Empedocles is a Hyperion who has eliminated the elements of Werther-like morbid sentimentality, who, by his sacrifice, consecrates his strength and does not confess his weakness; he is "the man of ripe experience, the mythical hero of antiquity, wise and sure of himself, for whom voluntary death is an act of faith proving the force of his wisdom." [1] Death in the flame is the least lonely of deaths. It is truly a cosmic death in which a whole universe is reduced to nothingness along with the thinker. The funeral pyre accompanies him in his passing.

> Giova cio solo che non muore, e solo
> Per noi non muore, cio che muor con noi.
>
> Only that is good which does not die, and only,
> For us, that does not die which dies with us.
>
> D'Annunzio

At times it is before an immense fire of live coals that the soul feels itself affected by the Empedocles complex. The Foscarina of D'Annunzio, burning with the inner flames of a hopeless love, desires death on the funeral pyre while, fascinated, she contemplates the furnace of the glass-blower: [2] " 'To disappear, to be swallowed up, to leave no trace!' moaned the heart of the woman intoxicated with the idea of destruction. 'In a second this fire could devour me like a vine twig, like a wisp of straw.' And she would approach the open apertures through which the liquid flames could be seen shining more brightly than summer's noon-day sun and coiling around the clay pots in which was melting the still shapeless metal that the workers, stationed about the furnace behind the firescreens, were scooping up with an iron rod in order to give it shape with the breath from their lips."

It can be seen that in the most varied circumstances the call of the funeral pyre remains a fundamental poetic theme. It no longer corresponds in modern life to any real-life observation. It does stir our emotions nonetheless. From Victor Hugo to Henri de Régnier, the funeral pyre of Hercules continues, like a natural symbol, to portray to us the destiny of mankind. That which is purely artificial insofar as objective knowledge is concerned remains then profoundly real and active for unconscious reveries. The dream is stronger than experience.

CHAPTER THREE

Psychoanalysis and Prehistory:

The Novalis Complex

Psychoanalysis has already been long engaged in the study of legends and mythologies. It has prepared for studies of this kind a working stock of explanations that are sufficiently rich to throw light upon the legends surrounding the conquest of fire. But what psychoanalysis has not yet completely systematized—although the works of C. G. Jung have cast a bright light upon this point—is the study of scientific explanations, of objective explanations, which purport to account for the discoveries of prehistoric man. In this chapter we shall bring together and complete the observations of C. G. Jung by calling attention to the weakness of rational explanations.

In the first place we must criticize the modern scientific explanations which seem to us quite inappropriate for prehistoric discoveries. These scientific explanations originate in an arid and cursory rationalism which claims to be profiting by recurring factual evidence; but which is, however, quite unrelated to the *psychological* conditions of the primitive discoveries. There is then a place, we feel, for an indirect and secondary psychoanalysis which would constantly seek the unconscious under the conscious, the subjective value under the objective evidence, the reverie beneath the experiment. One can study only what one has first dreamed about. Science is formed rather on a reverie than on an experiment, and it takes a good many experiments to dispel the mists of the dream. It should be noted particularly that the same action working on the same substance to give the same objective result does not have the same objective meaning in mentalities as different as those of the primitive man and the educated modern man. For primitive man thought is a centralized reverie; for the educated modern man reverie is a loose form of thought. The dynamic meaning is completely opposite in the two cases.

For example, it is a leitmotiv of the rationalist explanation that the first men produced fire by the rubbing together of two pieces of dry wood. But the *objective* reasons that are invoked to explain how men are supposed to have been led to imagine this procedure are very weak. These writers often do not even venture to try and throw light upon the psychology of this first discovery. Among the few authors who do concern themselves with an explanation, most recall that forest fires are produced by the "rubbing together" of branches in summer. They are applying just that recurrent rationalism that we wish to expose. They are judging by inference from a known science without seeking to recapture the conditions of the primitive observation. Nowadays, when people cannot discover another cause of a forest fire, they end by thinking that the unknown cause may be the action of rubbing. But in fact we can say that *the phenomenon in its natural aspect has never been observed.* If one were to observe it, it would not be, properly speaking, a rubbing action that one would think of if one approached the phenomenon from an ingenuous standpoint. One would think rather of a *shock*; one would find nothing that might suggest a phenomenon which is so prepared, long-lasting and progressive as the rubbing which is to cause the igniting of the wood. We arrive, then, at this critical conclusion: none of the practices based on rubbing that are used by primitive peoples to produce fire can be directly suggested by a phenomenon of nature.

These difficulties had not escaped Schlegel. Without putting forward any solution, he had seen quite clearly that the problem set forth in rational terms did not correspond to the psychological possibilities of primitive man.[1]

The mere invention of fire, the cornerstone of the whole cultural edifice, as the fable of Prometheus so well expresses it, presents insurmountable difficulties in our conjectures about man in a crude state of civilization. For us nothing is more common than fire; but man could have wandered in the desert for millions of years without once having seen fire on earthly soil. Let us grant him an erupting volcano, a forest set on fire by lightning: hardened in his nakedness against the rigors of the seasons, would he have run forward at once to warm himself? Would he not rather have taken flight? The sight of fire frightens most animals, except those which through a domesticated life have become accustomed to it . . . Even after having experienced the beneficient effect of a fire offered him by nature, how would he have been able to keep it going? Once extinguished, how would he have been able to rekindle it? Even if two pieces of dry wood had fallen for the first time into the hands of the savage, what previous experience would indicate to him that they could be ignited by a long-continued and rapid rubbing action?

On the other hand, if a rational and objective explanation is really quite unsatisfactory in accounting for a discovery made by a primitive mind, a psychoanalytical explanation, however overbold it may seem, must in the end be the true psychological explanation.

In the first place it must be recognized that rubbing is a highly sexualized experience. Merely by glancing through the psychological documents amassed by classical psychoanalysis one will have no difficulty in convincing oneself of this fact. Secondly, one need only make a systematic study of the items of information gained by a special psychoanalysis of the impressions pertaining to heat, to be convinced that the *objective* attempt to produce fire by rubbing is suggested by entirely intimate experiences. In any case, it is in this direction that the circuit between the phenomenon of fire and its reproduction is the shortest. The love act is the first scientific hypothesis about the objective reproduction of fire. Prometheus is a vigorous lover rather than an intelligent philosopher, and the vengeance of the gods is the vengeance of a jealous husband.

As soon as one has formulated this psychoanalytical observation, a great number of legends and customs are easily explained; curious expressions that have been unconsciously mingled with rational explanations appear in a new light. Thus Max Muller, who brought such a penetrating psychological intuition to the study of human origins, comes quite close to the psychoanalytical intuition without, however, actually discerning it.[2] "There were so many things to relate about fire!" And here then is the first: "It was the son of two pieces of wood." Why the *son*? Who is fascinated by this genetic point of view? Primitive man or Max Muller? In what way is such an image clearest? Is it clear objectively or subjectively? Where is the experience which throws light upon it? Is it the objective experience of the rubbing together of two pieces of wood or is it the intimate experience of a more gentle, more caressing kind of rubbing which excites the body of the beloved? One has only to ask these questions in order to disclose the source of the conviction which believes that fire is the son of wood.

Should we be surprised that this impure fire, the fruit of a secret love, should already be marked almost from its inception with the Oedipus complex? The expression of Max Muller is revealing in this regard: the second thing to be related about primitive fire was "how, no sooner had it been born, than it devoured its father and mother, that is to say the two pieces of wood from which it had sprung." Never has the Oedipus complex been better and more completely revealed: if you lack fire, this *burning* failure will gnaw at your heart, the fire will remain within you. If you produce fire, the sphinx itself will consume you. Love is but a fire that is to be transmitted. Fire is but a love whose secret is to be detected.

Since Max Muller naturally was not able to profit by the new knowledge provided by the psychological revolution of the Freudian era, certain inconsistencies may be noted even in his linguistic thesis. He wrote, for example: "And when primitive man *pictured* fire and named it what must have happened? He could name it only according to what it did; it was that which consumed and that which gave light." One should expect then in following the *objective* explanation of Max Muller that it should be the *visual* attributes that are used to designate a phenomenon thought of by primitive man as something *visible*, always seen before being touched. But this is not the case: for according to Max Muller "it was particularly the rapid movement of the fire that caught man's attention." And thus it was called "the quick, the ag-ile, Ag-nis, ig-nis." This designation by an associated phenomenon that is objectively indirect and inconstant cannot fail to appear quite artificial. On the other hand the psychoanalytical explanation straightens everything out. Yes, fire is the Ag-nis, the Ag-ile, but what is originally agile is the *human* cause prior to the produced phenomenon; it is the hand which pushes the wooden stick through the groove, thereby imitating more intimate caresses. Before being the son of wood, fire is the son of man.

The generally accepted method of throwing light upon the psychology of prehistoric man is to study still existing primitive peoples. But for a psychoanalysis of objective knowledge there are other instances of *primitiveness* which seem to us to be ultimately more pertinent. Indeed, we need only consider a *new* phenomenon to verify the difficulty of adopting a truly adequate objective attitude. It seems that the *unknown* aspect of the phenomenon is actively and positively opposed to its objectivation. To the *unknown* aspect it is not so much ignorance which corresponds as error, and error that is most heavily overladen with subjective defects. In order to construct a psychology of *primitiveness* it is sufficient, then, to consider an essentially new piece of scientific knowledge and to follow the reactions of non-scientific, ill-educated minds that are ignorant of the methods of effective scientific discovery. The science of electricity in the eighteenth century offers us in this respect an indispensable mine of psychological observations. It should be particularly noted that *electrical fire*, even more perhaps than ordinary fire, which had then been relegated to the status of a banal phenomenon without psychoanalytical interest, was a *sexualized fire*. Since it is mysterious, it is clearly sexual. Concerning the idea of friction, of which we have just pointed out the obvious primary sexuality, we shall again find applied to electricity all that we have said about fire. Charles Rabiqueau, "Lawyer, engineer, holder of the King's privilege for all his works on Physics and Mechanics," wrote in 1753 a treatise on "The Spectacle of Elementary Fire or A Course in Experimental Electricity" (*Le spectacle du feu élémentaire ou Cours d'électricité expérimentale*). In this work one can see a kind of reciprocal of the psychoanalytical thesis that we are putting forward in this chapter to explain the production of fire by friction. Since friction is the cause of electricity, Rabiqueau will develop an *electrical theory of the sexes* on this theory of friction:

The gentle rubbing separates the parts composed of spirits of air which are opposed to the passage and the fall of a spirituous substance that we call seminal fluid. This electrical friction or rubbing arouses within us a sensation, a tickling through the sharpness of the points of the spirit of fire in proportion as the rarefaction takes place and this spirit of fire is accumulated at the place being rubbed. Then the liquid, unable to maintain the lightness of the spirit of fire accumulated in the atmosphere, leaves its place and comes to fall in the womb in which there is also atmosphere: the vagina is merely the pipe leading to the general reservoir formed by the womb. There is in the feminine sex a sexual part. This part is to that sex what the sexual part of man is to the man. This part is subject to a similar rarefaction, tickling and sensation. This same part also participates in the rubbing action. The points of the spirit of fire are felt even more by the feminine sex . . .

The feminine sex is the depository of the tiny human spheres which are in the ovaries. These little spheres are an electrical substance, inert and lifeless; like an unlit candle or an egg ready to receive the spark of life, or the pip of an apple or a seed: or finally, like the flint or match which awaits the spirit of fire . . .

We have perhaps already tired the patience of our reader; but similar texts, which could be extended and multiplied, tell us quite clearly of the secret preoccupations of a mind which claims to be devoting itself to "pure mechanics." One can see, moreover, that the center of the convictions is not at all the objective experiment. Everything that rubs, that burns, or that electrifies is immediately considered capable of explaining the act of generation.

When the unconscious secret harmonics of rubbing are lacking, when they have a poor resonance in dry and austere souls, immediately the act of rubbing, restored to its purely mechanical aspect, loses its power of explanation. From this point of view one could perhaps account for, psychoanalytically, the protracted resistance encountered by the kinetic theory of heat. This theory, very clear to the conscious understanding, entirely adequate for a mind that is sincerely positivistic, appears to be lacking in depth—we should really say lacking in unconscious satisfaction—to a prescientific mind. The author of an *Essay on the Cause of Electricity* (*Essai sur la cause de l'électricité*), addressed in a series of letters to G. Watson, reveals in these terms his disillusionment: "I find nothing to be so incorrectly reasoned as the statement that fire is caused by rubbing. It seems to me that one might just as well say that water is caused by the pump."

As for Mme du Châtelet, she does not appear to find in this thesis the slightest enlightenment and is content to admit that fire is a miracle: "It is undoubtedly one of the greatest miracles of Nature that the most violent Fire can be produced in a moment by the striking together of bodies that have the coldest appearance." Thus a fact which is plainly evident to a scientific mind grounded in the teaching of modern energetics and which can understand immediately that the sudden tearing away of a flint particle can lead to its incandescence, is an object of mystery for the prescientific mind of Mme du Châtelet. She needs a substantialist explanation, a *profound* explanation. *Profoundness* is something one hides; it is something one says nothing about. One is always justified in being preoccupied with it.

Our theory would appear less daring if the reader would only free himself from an intransigent utilitarianism and would cease to imagine prehistoric man as being automatically subject to misfortune and necessity. It is in vain that all travellers tell us about the carefree life of primitive man: we nevertheless continue to shudder at our mental picture of life at the time of the cave man. Perhaps our ancestor was more receptive to pleasure, more conscious of his happiness in proportion as he was less sensitive to suffering. The warm sense of well-being arising from physical love must have been transferred into many primitive experiences. To set fire to the stick by sliding it up and down in the groove in the piece of dry wood takes time and patience. But this work must have been very agreeable to an individual whose reverie was wholly sexual. It was perhaps while engaged in this gentle task that man learned to sing. In any case it is an obviously rhythmic kind of task, a task which *answers* to the rhythm of the worker, which brings him lovely, multiple resonances: the arm that rubs, the pieces of wood that strike together, the voice that sings, all are united in the same harmony and the same rhythmic increase in energy; everything converges on to the one hope, on to an objective whose *value* is known. As soon as one engages in the action of rubbing, one experiences a pleasant objective warmth at the same time that one has the warm impression of an agreeable form of exercise. The rhythms are mutually supporting. They are mutually induced and continue through self-induction. If we accepted the psychological principles of rhythm analysis of M. Pinheiro dos Santos, who advises us to give *temporal reality* only to that which vibrates, we would understand immediately the value of the vital dynamism and of the psychic totality attached to such a rhythmic task. It is really the whole being that is engaged in play. It is in this play rather than in some form of suffering that the primitive being finds self-awareness, which in the first place is self-confidence.

The way we imagine is often more instructive than what we imagine. One has only to read the account of Bernardin de Saint-Pierre to be struck by the readiness—and consequently by the sympathy—with which this writer "understands" the primitive method of obtaining fire by friction. Lost in the forest with Virginie, Paul wishes to give to his companion the "prickly cabbage" which is at the top of a young palmetto or cabbage palm. But the tree defies the axe, and Paul has no knife! Paul thinks of setting fire to the base of the tree, but he has no tinder box. Moreover, on this rock-covered island there are no flint-stones to be found. We note these rapid sentences full of ideas and second thoughts which denote that the various methods are being discarded as unfeasible. These sentences prepare psychoanalytically for the decision: I must resort to the method used by the blacks. This method will reveal itself as being so easy that we are surprised at the hesitations that preceded its adoption.[3]

With the sharp corner of a stone he made a little hole in a branch of well-dried wood and then placed this branch firmly beneath his feet; then with the cutting edge of this stone he made a point on another branch that was equally dry but of a different kind of wood. He then put this piece of pointed wood into the little hole of the branch that was under his feet and made it rapidly revolve between his hands as one rolls or rotates a beater with which one wishes to whip up chocolate. In a very few moments he caused smoke and sparks to rise up from the point of contact. He gathered dry grasses and other branches and set fire to the foot of the palmetto tree, which, soon after, fell with a great crash. He also made use of the fire to strip off from the cabbage fruit its envelope of long, prickly, fibrous leaves. Virginie and he ate part of this cabbage raw and the other part cooked under the embers and found both equally tasty . . .

One will notice that Bernardin de Saint-Pierre recommends using two pieces of wood of a *different nature*. For a primitive mind this difference is of a sexual order. In his *Voyage en Arcadie* Bernardin de Saint-Pierre will specify quite gratuitously the ivy and the laurel. We should also note that the comparison of the rubbing stick and the beater used to whip up chocolate is found in the *Physics* of the Abbé Nollet whose work Bernardin de Saint-Pierre, impelled by his scientific pretentions, used to read. This mixing of his dream and his reading is in itself symptomatic of a rationalization. Moreover, at no time does the writer appear to have seen the illogical elements in his story. An agreeable fancy carries him along, his unconscious rediscovers the joys of the first fire to be lit in a carefree atmosphere of mutual love.

Furthermore, it is quite easy to establish that the *eurhythmy* of an active rubbing motion, on condition that it be sufficiently gentle and prolonged, brings about a *euphoria*. One has only to wait until the violent acceleration has settled down, until the different rhythms are coordinated, to see the smile and the look of peace return to the face of the worker. This joy cannot be explained objectively. It is the indication of a specific affective power. In this way is explained the joy of rubbing, cleaning, furbishing, and polishing that could not be adequately explained by the meticulous care taken by certain housewives. Balzac has pointed out in *Gobseck* that the "cold houses" of old maids had some of the shiniest furniture. Psychoanalytically speaking, cleanliness is really a form of uncleanliness.

In their parascientific theories, certain minds do not hesitate to accentuate the value given to the act of rubbing by going beyond the stage of solitary thoughts of love consisting wholly of reverie until they reach the circumstances of shared physical love. J.-B. Robinet, whose books went through a great number of editions, wrote in 1766: "The flintstone that is being rubbed in order to make it luminous understands what is being demanded of it, and its brilliance proves its condescension . . . I cannot believe that minerals should do us so much good through their virtues without enjoying the sweet satisfaction, the gentle satisfaction which is the first and greatest reward for beneficence." Opinions that are objectively so absurd must have a deep-rooted psychological cause. Sometimes Robinet breaks off his explanations for fear of "exaggerating." A psychoanalyst would say "for fear of betraying himself." But the exaggeration is already quite obvious. It is a psychological fact that has to be explained. We do not have the right to overlook it, as would a history of science that was systematically devoted to objective results.

To sum up then, we propose, as did C. G. Jung, to seek out systematically the component elements of the Libido in all primitive activities. Indeed, it is not only in art that the Libido is sublimated. It is the source of all the works of *homo faber*.

Someone undoubtedly stated it very well when he defined man as: a hand and a language. But the *useful* gestures must not hide the *agreeable* gestures. The hand is the organ that caresses, just as the voice is the organ that sings. Primitively, caress and work must have been associated. Long tasks are relatively easy tasks. A traveller tells us about primitive men shaping objects on the polishing wheel in a work which might last for two months. The more gentle the retouching instrument, the finer is the polish. In a somewhat paradoxical way we might well state that the age of chipped stone is the age of the tormented stone, whereas the age of the polished stone is the age of the caressed stone. The brutish man breaks the silex or flint, he does not work at it. The man who works at the silex loves the silex, and one does not love stones any differently than one loves women. When we look at an axe of dressed flint, it is impossible to resist the idea that each well-placed facet was obtained by a *reduction* in force, by an inhibited, restrained, directed force, in short, by a psychoanalyzed force. With the polished stone, we pass from the intermittent caress to the continued caress, to the gentle, the enveloping, the rhythmic and seductive movement. In any case, the man who works away with such patience is encouraged both by a memory and by a hope, and it is in the domain of the affective powers that we must look for the secret of his reverie.

The mark of a distinctive ceremony is forever attached to the production of fire by friction. In the fire rituals that were so famous in the Middle Ages and are so universally in evidence among primitive tribes, a return is sometimes made to the initial custom, a fact which seems to prove that the birth of fire is the primary cause of its adoration. In Germania, according to A. Maury, the Nothfeuer or Nodfyr had to be lit by rubbing two pieces of wood together. Chateaubriand gives us a long description of the ceremony of the *new fire* among the Natchez. On the night preceding the ceremony, the fire, which has been burning for a whole year, is allowed to go out. Before dawn appears, the priest slowly rubs two pieces of wood together while pronouncing in a low voice some magic words. When the Sun appears, the priest speeds up the motion. "At that moment the High Priest utters the sacred 'oah,' fire spurts forth from the wood which has been heated by the friction, the tinder which has been treated with sulphur catches fire . . . The medicine man sets fire to the hoops of reed: the flame winds along following their spiral shapes. Pieces of oak bark are kindled upon the altar, and this new fire then gives a new seed to the extinguished hearths of the village." [4] Thus this festival among the Natchez, which unites the Sun festival and the harvest festival, is above all a celebration of the *seeding* of the fire. In order that it may have all its force, this seeding must be seized in its first intensity, when it comes fresh from the rubbing tool which causes the fire. The method of rubbing then appears as the *natural* method. Once again it is natural because man accedes to it *through his own nature.* In actual fact, fire was detected within ourselves before it was snatched from the gods.

Frazer gives numerous examples of bonfires that are kindled through friction. Among others the Scottish fires of Beltane were lit by *forced* fire or *need-fire.*[5] "This was a fire produced exclusively by the rubbing of two pieces of wood against one another. As soon as the first sparks were emitted, they applied a species of agaric which grows on old birch trees and is very combustible. This fire had the appearance of being immediately derived from heaven and manifold were the virtues ascribed to it. They esteemed it . . . a sovereign remedy against malignant diseases, both in men and in cattle . . ." One wonders to what "appearance" Frazer is alluding when he says that *this forced fire descends directly* from heaven. But on this point Frazer's whole system of explanation seems to us to be misdirected. Frazer indeed bases his explanations on *utility*. Thus from the bonfires are taken ashes which go to fertilize the fields of flax, wheat and barley. This first proof introduces a sort of *unconscious rationalization* which misleads a modern reader who is easily convinced of the usefulness of carbonates and other chemical fertilizers. But let us look more closely at how these facts lead us to profound and obscure values. These ashes from the forced fire are given not only to the land which is to yield the harvests, but are also mixed in with the cattle fodder to make the animals fat. Sometimes they are mixed in so that the cattle will multiply. Now the psychological reason for the custom becomes obvious. Whether an animal is being fed or fields are being fertilized, there is, over and above the evident utility, a more intimate dream, the dream of fertility in its most sexual form. The ashes of the bonfires make fertile both animals and fields, *because* they make women fertile. It is the experience of the flame of love which forms the basis for the objective induction. Once more the explanation by the *useful* must give way to the explanation by the *agreeable*, the rational explanation must give way to the psychoanalytical explanation. When the accent is placed, as we propose to do, on the agreeable value, it must be granted that while the fire is *useful afterwards*, it is already agreeable in its preparation. It is perhaps more enjoyable before than after, like love. At the very least the happiness that results is subordinate to the happiness that is first sought. And if the primitive man is convinced that the bonfire, the originating fire, has all kinds of virtues and that it gives both power and health, it is because he experiences the well-being, the inner and almost invincible strength of the man who is living that decisive moment when the fire is about to shine forth and his desires to be fulfilled.

But we must go even further, it seems, and reverse Frazer's explanation in every detail. For Frazer, the bonfires are ceremonies connected with the death of the vegetation divinities, particularly the forest vegetation. One may then wonder why these gods of vegetation should hold such an enormous place in the primitive mind. What then is the first *human* function of the woods: is it shade; is it the rare and sickly fruit? Is it not rather the fire? And here is the dilemma: do they make fires in order to worship the woods, as Frazer believes, or do they burn the wood in order to worship the fire, as a more profoundly animistic explanation would have it? It seems to us that this latter interpretation casts a good deal of light upon details of the *fire festivals* which remain unexplained in Frazer's interpretation. Thus why does tradition often recommend that bonfires should be lighted by a young girl and a young man together; or by that man among the inhabitants of the village who was last married? Frazer pictures all the young people "jumping over the glowing embers in order to obtain a good harvest, or in order to make within the year a good marriage, or again in order to avoid attacks of colic." Among these three motives is there not one which for youth is clearly predominant? Why is it "the youngest married woman of the village who is to jump over the fire?" Why, in Ireland, "when a girl jumps three times forwards and backwards over a fire, do they say that she will soon be married, that she will be happy and that she will have a great many children?" Why are certain young people "convinced that the Saint John's fire will not burn them?" Do they not, in order to establish such a strange conviction, have an experience that is more intimate than objective? And how do the Brazilians place "red-hot coals in their mouths without burning themselves?" What then is this initial experience which inspired them with this audacity? Why do the Irish cause "to pass through the fires of the solstice those of their cattle which were sterile?" And this legend of the valley of Lech is very clear also: "When a young man and a young woman jump together over one of these fires without being touched even by the smoke, they say that the young woman will not be a mother during the year because the flames have neither touched her nor made her fertile." She has shown that she had the skill to play with fire without being burnt. Frazer wonders whether one could not attach to this latter belief "the scenes of debauchery in which the Estonians engage on the day of the solstice." And yet, in a book in which he does not hesitate to pile up references, he gives no account of this igneous debauch. Nor does he feel it necessary to give us a circumstantiated account of the fire festival in northern India, a festival "which is accompanied by singing and gestures which are licentious to the point of obscenity."

This last remark indicates certain drawbacks in his methods of explanation. We could have cited a large number of questions which remain unanswered in Frazer's theory but which are easily resolved by the theory of the primitive sexualization of fire. Nothing can make us better understand the inadequacy of sociological explanations than a parallel reading of Frazer's *The Golden Bough* and Jung's *Libido*. Even on an extremely precise point such as the problem of the mistletoe, the insight of the psychoanalyst appears to be decisive. One will find, moreover, in Jung's book numerous arguments in support of our thesis concerning the sexual nature of rubbing and of primitive fire. We have merely systematized these arguments and added to them certain documents drawn from a mental zone which is less profound and therefore closer to that of objective knowledge.

That particular book of Frazer which is entitled *Myths of the Origin of Fire* reveals on each page such obviously sexual marks that a psychoanalysis of it is really unnecessary. Since our aim in this short book is rather to study modern mentalities, we shall not dwell upon the primitive mentalities studied by Frazer. We shall, therefore, give only a few examples to illustrate the necessity for correcting the sociologist's interpretation by a psychoanalytical interpretation.

Often the creator of fire is a little bird bearing on its tail a red mark which is the mark of fire. In one Australian tribe the legend is very amusing or, rather, it is because a bird is being amusing that it succeeds in stealing the fire. "The deaf adder had formerly the sole possession of fire, which he kept securely in his inside. All the birds tried in vain to get some of it, until the small hawk came along and played such ridiculous antics that the adder could not keep his countenance and began to laugh. Then the fire escaped from him and became common property."[6] Thus, as is often the case, the legend of fire is the legend of licentious love. Fire is associated with innumerable jokes.

In many cases the fire is *stolen*. The Prometheus complex is dispersed over all the animals in creation. The one stealing the fire is most often a bird, a wren, a robin, a hummingbird, some small creature. Sometimes it is a rabbit, a badger, or a fox who carries off the fire at the end of its tail. Elsewhere women fight one another: "finally one of the women breaks her cudgel and immediately there comes forth from it fire." Fire is also produced by an old woman who "vented her rage by breaking off two sticks from the trees and rubbing them violently together." [7] On several occasions the creation of fire is associated with a similar act of violence: fire is the objective phenomenon of an inner rage, of a hand which has become irritable. It is thus quite noteworthy that we always come upon an exceptional psychological condition that is strongly tinged with affectivity at the origin of an objective discovery. We can distinguish then between many kinds of fire—gentle fire, cunning fire, unruly fire—by characterizing them according to the initial psychology of the desires and passions.

An Australian legend recalls that a totemic animal, a certain euro, carried fire within its body. A man killed it. "He examined the body carefully to see how the animal made fire, or where it came from; and pulling out the male organ of generation, which was of great length, he cut it open and found that it contained very red fire." [8] How could such a legend be perpetuated if it were not that each generation had its intimate reasons to believe in it?

In another tribe

> . . . the men had no fire and did not know how to make it, but the women did. While the men were away hunting in the bush, the women cooked their food and ate it by themselves. Just as they were finishing their meal, they saw the men returning away in the distance. As they did not wish the men to know about the fire, they hastily gathered up the ashes, which were still alight, and thrust them up their vulvas, so that the men should not see them. When the men came close up they said: "Where is the fire?" but the women replied: "There is no fire." [9]

In studying such a story, one must admit *the total impossibility of the realistic explanation,* whereas the psychoanalytical explanation is, on the contrary, immediately clear. It is quite evident, indeed, that one cannot hide *real* fire, *objective* fire, within the human body, as so many myths claim. It is equally true that it is only on the emotional level that one can lie with such effrontery and say, in the face of all the evidence, and by denying the most intimate form of desire, "There is no fire."

In a South-American myth, the hero, in order to get fire, pursues a woman:

He sprang up and seized her. He said that he would embrace her if she did not reveal to him the secret of fire. After several evasions, she consented to do so. She sat flat on the floor with legs wide apart. Taking hold of the upper part of her abdomen she gave it a good shake and a ball of fire rolled out of the genital canal on the floor. This was not the fire that we know today; it would not burn nor make things boil. These properties were lost when the woman gave it up. Ajijeko said, however, that he could remedy that; so he gathered all the bark, fruits, and hot peppers which burn, and with these and the woman's fire he made the fire that we now use.[10]

This example affords us definite evidence of the passing over from *metaphor to reality*. It should be noticed that this transition does not take place, as the realist explanation would have it, from reality to metaphor, but, in quite the opposite manner and in accord with the theory we are supporting, it proceeds from metaphors of subjective origin to an objective reality: the fire of love and the fire of pepper joined together end by setting fire to the dry grasses. It is this absurdity which explains the discovery of fire.

Generally speaking, one cannot read the rich and intensely interesting book of Frazer without being struck by the poverty of the realist explanation. There must be at least a thousand legends that are studied in the book and only two or three of these are explicitly connected with sexuality. For the rest, in spite of the underlying affective meaning, one might imagine that the myth has been created for the purpose of affording objective explanations. Thus, "the Hawaiian myth of the origin of fire, like many of the Australian myths of the same type, also serves to explain the particular color of a certain species of bird." Elsewhere the theft of fire by a rabbit served to explain the reddish-brown or black color of its tail. Such explanations, hypnotized by an objective detail, fail to take into account the primitivity of the *affective* interest. The primitive phenomenology is a phenomenology of affectivity: it fabricates objective beings out of phantoms that are projected by reverie, it creates images out of desires, material experiences out of somatic experiences, and fire out of love.

The Romantics, by returning to certain more or less permanent experiences of primitiveness, rediscovered, without suspecting it, those themes of fire that have been accorded a sexual value. G. H. von Schubert, for example, has written this sentence which only becomes clear in the light of a psychoanalysis of fire:[11] "Just as friendship prepares us for love, so by the rubbing together of similar bodies, nostalgia (heat) is created and love (flame) spurts forth." How can it be better stated that nostalgia is the memory of the warmth of the nest, the memory of the cherished love for the "calidum innatum." The poetry of the nest, of the fold, has no other origin. No objective impression acquired by examining the nests in a row of bushes could ever have supplied the wealth of adjectives which confer such a value upon the coziness, the sweetness, and the warmth of the nest. Were it not for the memory of man made warm by man, producing as it were a redoubling of *natural* heat, we could not conceive of lovers speaking of their snug little nest. Gentle heat is thus at the source of the consciousness of happiness. More precisely, it is the consciousness of the origins of happiness.

All of Novalis' poetry could receive a new interpretation, if we would apply to it the psychoanalysis of fire. This poetry is an attempt to re-live *primitivity*. For Novalis, the story is always more or less a cosmogony (theory of the formation of the universe). It is contemporaneous with a soul and a world that are being created. He maintains that the story is "the era . . . of liberty, the primitive state of nature, the age before the *Cosmos*."[12] Here, then, in all his obvious ambivalence, we see the *rubbing god* who is going to produce both fire and love: the beautiful daughter of King Arctur

> . . . lying on silken cushions, was reclining on a throne artistically carved from an enormous sulphur crystal; and some maid servants were energetically rubbing her delicate limbs which seemed a blend of milky whiteness and crimson.

And on all the places over which passed the hand of the servants there broke through the entrancing light with which the whole palace shone in such a marvellous manner . . .

This light is an inward light. The person being caressed shines with happiness. The caress is none other than the act of rubbing symbolized and idealized.

But the scene continues:

The hero remained silent.

"Let me touch your shield," she said sweetly,

and as he consented

. . . his whole armor vibrated; and an enlivening force ran through his whole body. His eyes flashed; his heart could be heard beating beneath its cuirass.

The beautiful Freya seemed more serene; and more burning did the light become which was emanating from her.

"The King is coming!" cried a wonderful bird . . .

If we add that this bird is the "phoenix," the phoenix which is reborn from its ashes, like a desire that has been momentarily appeased, we see, moreover, that this scene is marked by the double primitivity of fire and of love. If we set the beloved on fire when we love, this is proof that we ourselves loved when we kindled this fire.

"When Eros, transported with joy, saw that he was in front of the sleeping Freya, suddenly a sharp sound was heard. A powerful spark had run from the princess to his sword." The exact psychoanalytical image would have led Novalis to say "from the sword to the princess." In any case, "Eros dropped his sword. He ran to the princess and imprinted a kiss of fire on her cool lips." [13]

If from the work of Novalis we struck out the intuitions of primitive fire, it seems that all the poetry and dreams would be dissipated at the same time. The case of Novalis is so characteristic that it could be made the type example of a particular complex. In the field of psychoanalysis the naming of things is often sufficient to cause a *precipitate;* before the name, there was only an amorphous, troubled, disturbed solution; after the name, crystals are seen at the bottom of the liquid. The *Novalis complex* would synthesize, then, this impulse towards fire that is brought about by friction, the need for a shared warmth. This impulse would reconstitute, in its exact primitivity, the prehistoric conquest of fire. The Novalis complex is characterized by a consciousness of inner heat which always takes precedence over a purely visual knowledge of light. It is based upon a satisfaction of the thermal sense and the deep-seated consciousness of calorific happiness. Heat is a property, a possession. It must be guarded jealously and only given as a gift to a chosen being who merits its communion in a reciprocal fusion. Light plays upon and laughs over the surface of things, but only heat *penetrates*. In a letter to Schlegel, Novalis wrote: "You can see in my tale my antipathy for the play of light and shadow, and the desire for bright, hot, penetrating Ether."

This need to *penetrate*, to go to the *interior* of things, to the *interior* of beings, is one attraction of the intuition of inner heat. Where the eye cannot go, where the hand does not enter, there heat insinuates itself. This communion at the interior, this thermal sympathy, will, in the work of Novalis, find its symbol in the descent into the depths of the mountain, into the grotto and the mine. It is there that the heat is diffused and equalized, that it becomes indistinct like the contour of a dream. As Nodier has very well recognized, every description of a descent into hell has a dream structure.[14] Novalis has dreamed of the warm intimacy of the earth as others dream of a cold, resplendent, expanding sky. For him the miner is an "astrologer in reverse." Novalis lives with a concentrated heat rather than with a luminous radiation. How often he has meditated "on the edge of the dark abysses!" He is not the poet of minerals because he was a mining engineer; he became an engineer, although a poet, in order to obey the call of the subterranean, in order to return to the "calidum innatum." In his words, the miner is the hero of the depths, prepared "to receive the divine gifts and to exalt himself joyfully above the world and its miseries." The miner sings of the Earth: "To Her he feels bound—and intimately united

—and for Her he feels the same ardor as for a fiancée." The Earth is the maternal bosom, warm as a mother's lap in the unconscious mind of the child. The same heat animates both the rock and the miner's heart. "One would say that the miner has in his veins the inner fire of the earth which excites him to explore its depths."

At the center are the seeds; at the center is the engendering fire. That which germinates burns. That which burns germinates. " 'I need . . . flowers that have grown in the Fire . . . Zinc!' cried the King.[15] 'Give us flowers . . .' The gardener stepped out of the ranks, went to fetch a pot filled with flames and sowed in it a shining seed. It was not long before the flowers sprang forth . . ."

Perhaps a positive-minded person will undertake to develop here a *pyrotechnical* interpretation. He will show us the brilliant flame from the zinc projecting the white and dazzling flakes of its oxide into the air. He will write down the oxidation formula. But this *objective* interpretation, while it discovers a chemical cause of the phenomenon that fills us with wonder, will never take us to the center of the image, to the kernel of the Novalis complex. This interpretation will even deceive us as to what kinds of imagery take precedence in the poet's mind; for, by following this particular interpretation, we shall not understand that for a poet like Novalis the need to feel dominates the need to see, and that ahead of the light of Gœthe there must be placed the gentle, indistinct heat that is ingrained in all the fibres of the being.

No doubt there are more subdued tones in the work of Novalis. Often love gives way to nostalgia just as it does in the work of von Schubert; but the mark of heat is indelibly stamped upon it. You may also object that Novalis is the poet "of the little blue flower," the poet of the forget-me-not tossed as a pledge of imperishable memory over the edge of the precipice in the very shadow of death. But go down into the depths of the unconscious, find there with the poet the primitive dream and you will clearly see the truth: the little blue flower is red!

CHAPTER FOUR

Sexualized Fire

If the conquest of fire was originally a sexual "conquest," it is not surprising that fire should have remained so strongly sexualized for such a long period of time. As a result fire has received a whole series of values which greatly interfere with any objective investigations into the subject. Thus, before dealing with the chemistry of fire in the next chapter, we shall first demonstrate the necessity for a psychoanalysis of objective knowledge. The sexualized values that we wish to expose may be either hidden or explicit. Naturally it is the secret and obscure values which are most proof against psychoanalysis, but at the same time they are the most active. Openly acknowledged sexual values are immediately reduced by ridicule. In order that we may indicate clearly the *resistance* offered by the deeply hidden unconscious values, we shall give some examples in which this resistance is so weak that the reader can smilingly make the reduction himself without our having to call attention to the obvious errors.

In the opinion of Robinet[1] [writing in the mid-eighteenth century], elementary fire is capable of *reproducing* its own kind. This is a hackneyed, valueless expression that usually passes unnoticed. But Robinet ascribes to it its strong, primary meaning. He thinks that *the element of fire is born of a specific germ.* Thus, like any power which engenders, fire can be stricken with sterility as soon as it reaches a certain age. From now on, without apparently having any knowledge of tales concerning the festival of new fire or of restored fire, Robinet, in his reverie, will rediscover the *genetic necessity* for fire. If fire is left to live its natural life, even though it be fed, it grows old and dies like plants and animals.

Naturally the various fires must bear the indelible mark of their own individuality:[2] "Common fire, electrical fire, the fires of phosphorus, of volcanoes and of thunderbolts have essential, intrinsic differences that it is natural to ascribe to a more internal principle than to mere accidents that may be presumed to have modified the same igneous matter." There can be seen already at work the intuition of a substance that is understood as having an intimacy and a life of its own and will soon be attributed its own power of generation. Robinet continues: "Each thunderbolt could well be the effect of a new production of igneous Beings, which, increasing rapidly in size, because of the abundance of vapors which feed them, are collected by the winds and carried back and forth through the middle regions of the atmosphere. The many new volcanoes in America, the new eruptions of the old craters, also give proof of the productiveness and the fecundity of the subterranean fires." Certainly this fecundity is not a metaphor. It must be taken in its most precise sexual meaning.

These igneous beings, born of the Thunderbolt, in a flash of lightning, escape observation. But Robinet claims to have precise observations at his disposal:[3] "Hooke, having struck a flint over a sheet of paper and having examined with a good microscope the spots where the sparks had fallen, which were marked by little black specks, observed there some round and shiny atoms, although the naked eye could see nothing. They were little shiny worms."

Does not the life of the fire, made up entirely of sparks and sudden flickerings, remind us of the life of the ant heap? "At the slightest incident, the ants can be seen swarming tumultuously out of their underground dwelling: similarly, at the slightest shock to the piece of phosphorus, the igneous animalculae can be seen to collect and come forth with a luminous appearance."

Finally, life alone is capable of supplying a *profound inner* reason for the obvious individuality of colors. To explain the seven colors of the spectrum Robinet does not hesitate to propose "seven ages or periods in the life of the igneous animalculae . . . These animals, in passing through the prism, will each be obliged to suffer refraction according to its strength and age and thus each will bear its own color." Is it not true that the dying fire turns red? For anyone who has tried to start up a lazy fire by blowing on it there is a very clear distinction between the recalcitrant fire which is *dying down* to a red glow and the young fire which, as an alchemist puts it so prettily, strives to attain "the brilliant redness of the rustic poppy." Faced with a dying fire, the man who is doing the blowing becomes discouraged; he no longer feels sufficient ardor to communicate his own power to the fire. If he is a realist like Robinet, he *realizes* his discouragement and his impotency; he makes a phantom of his own fatigue. Thus the mark of changeable man is placed upon things. That which diminishes or increases within ourselves becomes the sign of a life that is either stifled or fully awakened within reality. A poetic communion of such a nature lays the groundwork for the most tenacious errors as far as objective knowledge is concerned.

Moreover, as we have so often remarked, it would be necessary only to put this intuition, which is so ridiculous in the form given by Robinet, into a vague and imprecise form, to poeticize it and restore its subjective meaning, in order to have it accepted without difficulty. Thus, if these animated forms of color are regarded as powers imbued with an ardent or waning life, if they are created, not on the axis which proceeds from the objects to the eye, but on the axis of the passionate glance which projects a desire and a love, then they become the varied shades of love itself. Thus it is that Novalis can write:[4] "A ray of light can also be broken into something quite different from colors. At any rate the ray of light is capable of being endowed with life so that the soul meeting it feels itself assailed by many shades of feeling. In this respect do we not think of the rays from the eyes of our beloved?" If we reflect a moment, we will realize that Robinet merely accentuates and makes heavy an image that Novalis will tone down and restore to its ethereal form; but, in the unconscious, the two images appear to be of the same species, and the objective parody of Robinet merely enlarges the features of the inner reverie of Novalis. This parallel, which will seem incongruous to poetic souls, helps us, however, to make a reciprocal psychoanalysis of two dreamers placed at the antipodes of reality. It affords us an example of those forms mixed with desires which can produce poems as well as philosophies. The philosophy may be bad even though the poems are beautiful.

Now that we have given an illustration of an erroneous interpretation of the animistic and sexualized intuition of fire, we shall doubtless have a better understanding of the futility of those assertions that are constantly being repeated as eternal truths: fire is life; life is a fire. In other words we wish to denounce this false assurance which claims to connect fire and life.

At the source of this assimilation, there is, we believe, the impression that the spark, like the seed, is a small cause which produces a great effect. Hence an intense value is ascribed to the myth of the igneous power.

But let us begin by showing the equation of the seed and the spark and let us realize that, through the interplay of inextricable reciprocals, the seed is a spark and the spark is a seed. The one does not go without the other. When two intuitions are linked together as these are, the mind believes it is *thinking*, even though it is moving only from one metaphor to another. A psychoanalysis of objective knowledge consists precisely of throwing light upon these loose transpositions. In our opinion, one has merely to place them beside one another to see that they have no real foundation, but simply rest upon one another. Here is an example of that easy assimilation that we are criticizing:[5]

Let an enormous pile of charcoal be lighted with the feeblest kind of light, a dying spark . . . , two hours later will it not form just as considerable a blaze as if you had at once lit it with a fiery torch? That is the story of generation: the most delicate man provides sufficient fire to bring about generation, and, in the act of copulation, his fire is just as potent as that of the much stronger man.

And to think that such comparisons could satisfy these muddled thinkers! In point of fact, far from helping to understand phenomena, they constitute true obstacles to scientific culture.

Towards the same date, in 1771, a medical doctor develops a lengthy theory of human fertilization based on fire considered as a supreme possession and a generating force:[6]

The depression which follows the emission of the spermatic fluid at least indicates to us that at this moment we are undergoing the loss of an extremely ardent and active liquid. Should we place the blame upon the loss of a small quantity of that marrowy, palpable juice that is contained in the seminal vesicles? Would the bodily organism, for which it was already as if non-existent, immediately take note of the loss of such a humor? The answer is undoubtedly no. But it is not the same with the fiery substance of which we have only a certain amount and with which all the vital centers are in direct communication . . .

Thus to lose flesh, marrow, juice and fluid is of little importance. To lose the fire, the seminal fire, that is the great sacrifice. This sacrifice alone can engender life. One can see, moreover, how easily the unquestioned value of fire can be established.

Authors who are no doubt second-rate, but who for that very reason reveal to us more naively the sexual intuitions that have been attributed an unconscious value, sometimes develop a whole sexual theory based on themes that are specifically connected with heat—thereby proving the initial confusion that existed between the intuitions of semen and fire. Doctor Pierre-Jean Fabre, in 1636, thus sets forth his theory as to the birth of male and female children:

If the semen, which is one and the same in all its parts and of an identical constitution, is divided in the womb and one part withdrawn to the right and the other to the left side, the mere fact of the division of the semen causes such a difference in it . . . not only in form and figure, but in sex, that one side will be male and the other female. And it is from that part of the semen which has withdrawn to the right side, as being the part of the body which is hotter and more vigorous, which will have maintained the force and the vigor and heat of the semen, that a male child will come forth; and the other part, since it has retired to the left side which is the colder part of the human body, will then have received cold qualities which will have much diminished and lessened the vigor of the semen, so that from it there will come forth the female child which, however, in its first origin was all male.[7]

Before proceeding any further, need we call attention to the complete gratuitousness of such assertions, which have not the slightest relation to any *objective* experience whatsoever? One cannot even discover a pretext for this in *external* observation. Consequently where does such nonsense originate if not in an improper evaluation of the *subjective* phenomena attributed to fire? Fabre, moreover, substantializes by means of fire all the qualities of strength, courage, ardor and virility. "Women, because of this cold and humid constitution, are less strong than men, more timid and less courageous, because of the fact that strength, courage and action come from fire and air, which are the active elements; and therefore they are called male elements; and the other elements, water and earth, are called passive and female elements."

By bringing together so many of these ridiculous statements, we have tried to illustrate a state of mind which fully *realizes* the most insignificant metaphors. Nowadays, since the scientific mind has changed structure several times, it has become accustomed to such numerous transpositions of meaning that it is less often a victim of its own expressions. All the scientific concepts have been *redefined.* In our conscious lives we have broken off direct contact with the original etymologies. But the prehistoric mind, and *a fortiori* the unconscious, does not detach the word from the thing. If it speaks of a man as being full of fire, it wills something to be *burning* within him. If necessary, this fire will be kept burning by a drink. Every impression of comfort comes from a cordial. Every cordial is an aphrodisiac to the unconscious mind. Fabre does not think it impossible that "through proper food, conducive to building up a hot and dry constitution, the feeble heat of females may become so strong that it may be enabled to thrust outward the parts which its weakness had kept back within." For "women are men in a latent state because they have the male elements hidden within them." How better can it be stated that the principle of fire is the male activity and that this wholly physical activity, like an erection, is the principle of life? The image that men are merely women dilated by heat is easy to psychoanalyze. We should also note the loose association of the confused ideas of heat, food, and generation; those who wish male children "will endeavor to nourish themselves with all the good, hot, and igneous foods."

Fire governs the moral qualities as well as the physical. The shrewdness of a man comes from his hot temperament. "Here the Physiognomists are excellent; for when they see a thin man of a dry disposition, with a moderate-sized head, shining eyes, chestnut or black hair, and of average height and squarely built, they then declare that this man is prudent and wise and full of wit and shrewdness." On the other hand,

> . . . the big tall men are humid and mercurial; shrewdness, made up of wisdom and prudence, is never at its highest degree in these men; for the fire from whence come wisdom and prudence is never vigorous in such large and vast bodies, since it is wandering and diffused; and nothing in nature that is scattered and diffused is ever strong and powerful. Force needs to be compact and compressed; the strength of fire is seen to be all the stronger when it is compressed and contracted. Cannons demonstrate this fact . . .

Like any form of wealth, fire is dreamed of in its concentrated form. The dreamer wishes to enclose it in a small space the better to guard it. One whole type of reverie brings us back to a meditation on the concentrated. It is the revenge of the small over the great, the hidden over the manifest. To sustain a reverie of this kind, a prescientific mind, as we have just seen, causes the most incongruous images to come together—the dark-haired man and the cannon. As an almost constant rule, it is in the reverie about what is small and concentrated and not in the reverie about what is large that the mind that has long been pondering over things finally discovers the path which leads to scientific thought. In any case, the thought of fire, more than the thought of any other principle, follows the inclination of this type of reverie to dream of a concentrated power. In the world of objects, it is the homologue of the love reverie in the heart of a taciturn man.

That fire is the principle of all seed appears so true to a prescientific mind that the slightest external appearance is enough to prove it: thus for Count de La Cépède:[8] "The seminal dusts of plants are highly inflammable substances . . . that put forth by the plant named the lycopodium is a kind of sulphur." This is an assertion of a chemistry of surface and color that the slightest experiment carried out by an objective chemistry of the substance would have contradicted.

At times fire is the formal principle of individuality. An alchemist writing a *lettre philosophique* published in 1723 as a continuation to the *Cosmopolite*, explains to us that fire is not, properly speaking, a body, but rather the male principle which vitalizes the female substance. This female substance is water. Water in its elemental state "was cold, humid, crass, impure and murky, and in creation held the place of the female, just as fire, whose innumerable sparks could be likened to different males, contained all the shades required for the procreation of particular individuals. We can call this fire the form, and the water the substance, both of which are mixed together in the original chaos."[9] And the author refers us to Genesis. Here may be recognized in its obscure form the intuition made ridiculous by the *precise* images of Robinet. Thus we can see that as error becomes cloaked by the unconscious, as it loses its precise outline, it becomes more acceptable. It would require only one further step in this direction to attain the gentle safety of philosophical metaphors. To assert that fire is an *element* is, in our opinion, to set up sexual resonances; it is thinking of the substance in its propagation, in its *generation;* it is rediscovering the alchemistic inspiration which spoke of a water or an earth *elemented* by fire, of a substance that was *embryonized* by sulphur. But as long as one does not give a precise indication of this *element*, or a detailed description of the various phases of this *elementation*, one has the dual advantage of the touch of mystery and the force of the primitive image. If we next treat the fire which animates our heart and that which animates the world as being one and the same, it will now appear that our feeling of communion with things is so powerful and primitive that precise criticism is disarmed. But what are we really to think of a *philosophy of the element* which claims it is not subject to precise criticism and is satisfied with a general principle which, in each specific case, reveals itself to be heavily charged with primitive fallacies and as naive as a lover's dream?

We have tried to show in a previous book[10] that all Alchemy was penetrated by an immense sexual reverie, by a reverie of wealth and rejuvenation, by a reverie of power. We would now like to demonstrate that this *sexual reverie* is a *fireside reverie*. One could even say that alchemy *realizes* purely and simply the sexual characteristics of the fireside reverie. Far from being a *description* of the objective phenomena, it is an attempt to *inscribe* human love at the heart of things.

What may at first sight hide its psychoanalytical character is the fact that alchemy quickly took on an abstract aspect. The alchemists worked with the *enclosed fire*, the fire confined in a furnace. The images which are created so lavishly by open flames and which lead to a more free and winged kind of reverie, were now reduced and decolorized to the benefit of a more precise and concentrated dream. Let us then take a look at the alchemist at work beside his furnace in his underground workshop.

It has already been noted many times that several of the furnaces and retorts used by the alchemists had undeniable sexual shapes. Some authors explicitly point this out. Nicolas de Locques, "the spagyric doctor to His Majesty," writes in 1665,[11] "To whiten, digest, and thicken as in the preparation and confection of the Magisteries, the alchemists take a recipient in the form of the Breasts or in the form of the Testicles for the production of the masculine and feminine seed in the Animal, and they call this recipient a Pelican."[12] Of course this symbolic homology between the different alchemical containers and the different parts of the human body was generally prevalent, as we have pointed out elsewhere. But it is perhaps from the sexual aspect that this homology is clearest and most convincing. Here the fire, confined in the sexual retort, has been seized at its primary source: it then has its entire efficacy.

The technique, or rather the philosophy, of fire in the art of alchemy is, moreover, dominated by well-defined sexual specifications. According to an anonymous author writing at the end of the seventeenth century:[13] There are

> . . . three sorts of fire, the natural, the "innatural" and the unnatural. The natural is the masculine fire, the principal agent; but in order to obtain it the Artist must take great pains and use all his knowledge; for it is so torpid and so strongly concentrated within metals that it cannot be set into action without persistent effort. The "innatural" fire is the feminine fire and the universal dissolvent, nourishing bodies and covering with its wings the nudity of Nature. It is no less difficult to obtain than the natural fire. This feminine fire appears in the form of a white smoke, and it often happens that in this form it may disappear because of the negligence of the Artists. It is almost impalpable, although, through physical sublimation, it appears to be corporeal and resplendent. The unnatural fire is that which corrupts the chemical compound and which first has the power of dissolving that which Nature had strongly joined together . . .

Need we call attention to the feminine sign attached to smoke, "the inconstant wife of the wind," as Jules Renard calls it? Is not every veiled apparition considered feminine by virtue of this fundamental principle of unconscious sexualization: all that is hidden is feminine? The white lady who haunts the valley comes to visit the alchemist at night, beautiful as the imprecise image, changeable as a dream, fugitive as love itself. For a brief moment she enfolds the sleeping man in her caress: a too sudden breath and she evaporates. . . . So the chemist misses his reaction.

From the calorific point of view, the sexual distinction is quite clearly complementary. The feminine principle of things is a principle pertaining to surface and outer covering, a lap, a refuge, a gentle warmth. The masculine principle is a principle of the center, a principle of power, active and sudden as the spark and the power of will. The feminine heat attacks things from without. The masculine heat attacks them from within, at the very heart of the essential being. Such is the profound meaning of the alchemist's reverie. Moreover, to gain a clear understanding of this sexualization of the alchemist's fires and the clearly predominant value attached to the action of the masculine fire upon the germ, we must not lose sight of the fact that alchemy is uniquely a science engaged in by men, by bachelors, by men without women, by initiates cut off from normal human relationships in favor of a strictly masculine society. Alchemy does not receive the influence of the feminine reverie directly. Its doctrine of fire is thus strongly polarized by unsatisfied desires.

This inner, masculine fire, the object of the meditation of the lonely man, is naturally considered to be the most powerful fire. In particular it is the fire which can "open bodies." An anonymous author writing at the beginning of the eighteenth century presents very clearly the value placed upon the fire that is confined within matter. "Art, in imitation of Nature, opens a body by means of fire, but uses a much stronger fire than the Fire that is produced by the fire of confined flames." The superfire prefigures the superman. Conversely, the superman, in his irrational form, conceived of in order to claim a uniquely subjective power, is scarcely more than a superfire.

This "opening" of bodies, this possession of bodies from within, this *total* possession, is sometimes an obvious sexual act. It is performed, as certain alchemists say, with the Rod of Fire. Similar expressions and the figures which abound in certain books on alchemy leave no doubt as to the meaning of this kind of possession.

When fire is performing obscure functions, it is really surprising that the sexual images should remain so clear. Indeed the persistence of these images, in areas in which direct symbolization remains confused, proves the sexual origin of ideas about fire. To realize this we need only to read in the books on alchemy the long account of the *marriage* of Fire and Earth. We can explain this *marriage* from three points of view: in its material meaning, as historians of chemistry always do; in its poetic meaning as do literary critics; in its original and unconscious meaning, as we propose to do here. Let us bring these three explanations to bear on one particular point by taking the often quoted alchemic lines:

> If the fixed body you can dissolve,
> And cause the solute then to rise,
> And fix in a powder what has risen,
> For your pains you'll be consoled.

We can easily find chemical examples which will illustrate the phenomenon of an earth (chemical substance) dissolved in solution which is then sublimated by distilling the solution. If we "then clip the wings of the spirit," if we *sublimate*, we will have a pure salt, *the sky of the terrestrial mixture* (as the alchemists describe the essence of the substance). We will have effected a material marriage of sky and earth. According to the beautiful and meaningful expression we now have "Uranogaea, the Sky terra-fied or made earth."

Novalis will carry over the same theme into the world of amorous dreams:[14] "Who knows if our love will not some day become wings of flame which will carry us away into our heavenly land before old age and death can overtake us." But this vague aspiration has its opposite, and, in Novalis, Fable sees this clearly "looking through the fissure in the rock . . . at Perseus with his great iron buckler; the scissors flew of their own accord towards the buckler, and Fable begged him to clip the wings of the Spirit with these scissors, then, by means of his shield, to deign to immortalize the sisters and complete the great work. . . . (Then) there is no longer any flax to spin. The inanimate is once more without a soul. The animate will reign henceforth and will mold and make use of the inanimate. The interior is revealed and the exterior is hidden."

Beneath this rather strange poetry, which has no direct appeal to classical taste, there is in this page the profound trace of a sexual meditation of fire. After the desire, the flame must come forth, the fire must reach completion and the destinies be fulfilled. To do this the alchemist and the poet reduce and restrain the burning action of the light. They separate the sky from the earth, the ash from the sublimate, the outside from the inside. And when the hour of happiness is over, Tourmaline, the gentle Tourmaline, "carefully gathers the heaped-up ashes."

Sexualized fire is preeminently the connecting link for all symbols. It unites matter and spirit, vice and virtue. It idealizes materialistic knowledge; it materializes idealistic knowledge. It is the principle of an essential ambiguity which is not without charm, but which must be continually recognized and psychoanalyzed in order that we may criticize both the materialists and the idealists: "I am manipulating," says the Alchemist. "No, you are dreaming." "I am dreaming," says Novalis. "No, you are manipulating." The reason for such a profound duality is that fire is within us and outside us, invisible and dazzling, spirit and smoke.

If fire is so misleading and ambiguous, one should begin any psychoanalysis of objective knowledge by a psychoanalysis of the intuitions concerning fire. We are almost certain that fire is precisely the first object, the *first phenomenon*, on which the human mind *reflected;* among all phenomena, fire alone is sufficiently prized by prehistoric man to wake in him the desire for knowledge, and this mainly because it accompanies the desire for love. No doubt it has often been stated that the conquest of fire definitely separated man from the animal, but perhaps it has not been noticed that the mind in its primitive state, together with its poetry and its knowledge, had been developed in meditation before a fire. *Homo faber* is the man of surfaces, his mind is fixed on a few familiar objects, on a few crude geometric forms. For him the sphere has no center, it is simply the objective counterpart of the rounding gesture he makes with his cupped hands. On the other hand the *dreaming man* seated before his fireplace is the man concerned with inner depths, a man in the process of development. Or perhaps it would be better to say that fire gives to the man concerned with inner depths the lesson of an inner essence which is in a process of development: the flame comes forth from the heart of the burning branches. And thus we have this intuition of Rodin, quoted without comment by Max Scheler, doubtless because he failed to see its clearly primitive character:[15] "Each thing is merely the limit of the *flame* to which it owes its existence." Were it not for our conception of the inner, formative fire, of fire understood as the source of our ideas and our dreams, of fire considered as a seed, the usual concept of an objective and completely destructive flame could not explain the profound intuition of Rodin. In meditating upon this intuition, we realize that Rodin is, as it were, the sculptor of the inner depths and that he has managed in some way, in spite of the strict requirements of his art, to bring the inner features to the surface like the projection of a life, or a flame.

In view of these findings we should no longer be surprised that works dealing with fire should be so easily sexualized. D'Annunzio portrays Stelio who, in the glass works, is contemplating, in the annealing oven,

> the extension of the smelting oven, the shining vases, still slaves of the fire, still under its power . . . Later, the beautiful frail creatures would abandon their father, would detach themselves from him forever; they would grow cold, become cold gems, would lead their new life in the world, enter the service of pleasure-seeking men, encounter dangers, follow the variations in light, receive the cut flower or the intoxicating drink.[16]

Thus "the eminent dignity of the arts of fire" arises from the fact that their products bear the most profoundly human mark, the mark of primitive love. They are the works of a *father*. The forms created by fire are modelled more than any other, as Paul Valéry has so well pointed out, "in order to be caressed."[17]

But a psychoanalysis of objective knowledge must go beyond this. It must recognize that *fire is the first cause of the phenomenon.* Indeed, we cannot speak of a world of the phenomenon, of a world of the appearances, except in the presence of a world which *changes* in its appearances. Now, from the primitive point of view, only those changes that are caused by fire are the deep, striking, swift, marvellous and definitive changes. The alternation of night and day, the interplay of light and shadow, are superficial and fleeting aspects which do not disturb to any extent the routine knowledge of objects. The fact of their alternation nullifies their causal nature, as philosophers have pointed out. If the day is the father and the cause of night, the night is the mother and the cause of day. Movement itself arouses scarcely any reflection. The human mind did not begin its development like a class in physics. The fruit that falls and the stream that flows present no enigma to a primitive mind. Primitive man contemplates the brook without thinking:

> As a drowsy shepherd watches the water flow by.

But the changes wrought by fire are changes in substance: that which has been licked by fire has a different taste in the mouths of men. That which fire has shone upon retains as a result an ineffaceable color. That which fire has caressed, loved, adored, has gained a store of memories and lost its innocence. In slang "flambé" is synonomous with "dead and done for" and is used in place of an indecent word that is charged with sexuality. Through fire everything changes. When we want everything to be changed we call on fire. The first phenomenon is not only the phenomenon of the fire contemplated in all its life and brilliancy during an hour of leisure, it is also the phenomenon caused *by* the fire. The phenomenon caused by fire is the most perceptible of all; it is the one that must be most closely watched; it must be speeded up or slowed down; we must grasp the *point* (or exact degree) of fire which leaves a mark on a substance as we do the *instant* of love which leaves a mark on an existence. As Paul Valéry says, in the arts of fire,[18]

. . . there can be no giving up, no respite; no fluctuations in thought, courage or humor. These arts prescribe, in its most dramatic aspect, the close combat between man and form. Their essential agent, *fire*, is also the greatest enemy. It is an agent of redoubtable precision, whose marvellous action upon the substance offered to its heat is rigorously limited, threatened and defined by several physical or chemical *constants* that are difficult to observe. Any error is fatal: the piece is ruined. Whether the fire dies down or whether it blazes up, its caprice means disaster . . .

To this phenomenon *through* fire, to this most noticeable of all phenomena, which is marked, however, in the depths of the substance, a name must be given: the first phenomenon which merited man's attention was the *pyromenon* or product of fire. We shall now see how this fire product, which was so intimately understood by prehistoric man, has for centuries foiled attempts at explanation on the part of scientists.

CHAPTER FIVE

The Chemistry of Fire: *History of a False Problem*

In this chapter we shall apparently be changing the field of our study; we shall, in fact, attempt to study the efforts made by objective knowledge to explain the phenomena produced by fire, the pyromena. But in our opinion this problem is really not one of scientific history, for the scientific part of the problem is falsified by the importation of the values whose action we have demonstrated in the preceding chapters. As a result, we really have to deal only with the history of the *confusions* that have been accumulated in the field of science by intuitions about fire. These intuitions are *epistemological obstacles* which are all the more difficult to overcome since they are psychologically clearer. In perhaps a slightly roundabout way we are still dealing, then, with a psychoanalysis which is really continuous in spite of the difference in viewpoint. Instead of turning to the poet and the dreamer, this psychoanalysis pays particular attention to the chemists and the biologists of past centuries. But in so doing it discovers a *continuity* of thought and reverie, and observes that in this union of thought and of dreams it is always the thought that is twisted and defeated. Thus it becomes necessary, as we proposed in a preceding work, to psychoanalyze the scientific mind, to bind it to a discursive thought which, far from *continuing* the reverie, will halt it, break it down and prohibit it.

We have a ready proof that the problem of fire lends itself poorly to an historical treatment. Mr. J. C. Gregory has written a clear and intelligent history of the theories of combustion from Heraclitus to Lavoisier. Now this book *links* ideas with such rapidity that fifty pages suffice to tell of the "science" of twenty centuries. Moreover, if we take into account the fact that by the time of Lavoisier these theories were revealed to be objectively false, then a doubt must occur to us as to the *intellectual* nature of these doctrines. In vain it will be objected that the Aristotelian doctrines are plausible, that they can, with appropriate modifications, explain different stages of scientific knowledge, that they may be *adapted* to the philosophy of certain periods; the fact remains that one cannot determine the reason for the solidity and persistence of these doctrines merely by putting forward their value as objective explanations. We must go deeper beneath the surface; then we shall come upon the unconscious values. It is these unconscious values which make for the persistence of certain explanatory principles. By a gentle form of torture, Psychoanalysis must make the scientist confess his unavowable motives.

Fire is perhaps the phenomenon which has most preoccupied chemists. For a long time it was believed that to resolve the enigma of fire was to resolve the central enigma of the Universe. Boerhaave, writing about 1720, says:[1] "If you make a mistake in your exposition of the Nature of Fire, your error will spread to all the branches of physics, and this is because, in all natural production, Fire . . . is always the chief agent." A half-century later, Scheele recalls at one point,[2] "the innumerable difficulties presented by research into fire. It is frightening to think of the centuries that have elapsed without our succeeding in acquiring more knowledge as to its true properties." At another point he says:

Some persons fall into an absolutely opposite kind of error when they explain the nature and the phenomena of Fire with so much facility that it would seem that all difficulties have been solved. But how many objections could we not make to their theories? Here they say that heat is elementary Fire, soon it becomes an effective Fire: there, light is the purest form of Fire and an element; here, it is already spread throughout the whole extent of the globe, and the impulse of elementary Fire communicates to it its direct movement; there, light is an element which one can capture by means of the *acidum pingue*, and which is set free by the expansion of this supposed acid, etc.

This vacillation, so well indicated by Scheele, is very symptomatic of the dialectic of ignorance which proceeds from obscurity to utter blindness and which readily takes the very terms of the problem to be its solution. Since fire has not been able to reveal its mystery, they take it to be a universal cause: then everything is explained. The more untrained is a prescientific mind, the greater the problem it selects. About this great problem it will write a little book. The book of the marquise du Chàtelet is 139 pages long, and its subject is Fire.

In prescientific periods it is thus quite difficult to establish the bounds of one's subject of study. For fire, more than any other phenomenon, the animistic and the substantialistic conceptions are mingled in an inextricable fashion. Whereas in our general treatment we have been able to analyze these conceptions separately, we must here study them in their confused combined state. Whenever we have been able to go more deeply into our analysis, it has been precisely thanks to these scientific ideas which have allowed us gradually to discern errors. But fire has not yet found its own science as has electricity. It has remained in the prescientific mind as a complex phenomenon which is dependent both on chemistry and biology. In order that we may account for the phenomena of fire, we must then retain in our concept of fire the aggregate aspect that corresponds to the ambiguity of the explanations, which pass alternatively from life to matter in an interminable reciprocal motion.

Fire can then serve as an illustration for the theses that we put forward in our book, *The Formation of the Scientific Mind* (*La Formation de l'esprit scientifique*). In particular, through the naive ideas that have been developed about it, fire affords examples of the *substantialistic obstacle* and of the *animistic obstacle* which both impede scientific thought.

We shall first put forward cases in which the substantialist assertions are presented without the slightest proof. The Reverend Father L. Castel does not question the *realism of fire*:[3] "The dark colors used in painting are for the most part the products of fire, and fire always leaves something corrosive and burning in the bodies which have received its hot imprint. Some people claim that these are the igneous parts, composed of a true fire, that remain in different kinds of lime, in ashes, in coals and in various types of smoke." Nothing justifies this *substantial persistence* of fire in coloring matter, but the substantialist thought can be seen at work: that which has received fire must remain burning, and hence corrosive.

Sometimes the substantialist assertion is presented in untroubled purity, quite free from any attempt at proof and even from any illustrative image. Thus Ducarla writes:[4] "The igneous molecules . . . heat because they are; they are because they have been . . . This action never stops going on except for lack of an object." The tautological nature of the substantial attribution is here particularly clear. The joke of Molière about the dormitive virtues of opium which makes you sleep did not prevent an important, late eighteenth-century author from saying that the calorific virtue of heat has the property of heating.

For many minds, fire has such value that nothing limits its power. Boerhaave claims to make no assumption concerning fire, but he begins by stating without the least hesitation that "the elements of Fire are met everywhere; they are found in gold, which is the most solid of all known bodies, and in the vacuum of Torricelli." [5] For a chemist as for a philosopher, for an educated man as for a dreamer, fire is so easily endowed with a substance that it can be attached equally well to the vacuum as to the plenum. Doubtless modern physics will recognize that the vacuum is traversed by the thousand radiations of radiant heat, but it will not claim that these radiations are a quality of empty space. If a light is produced in the vacuum of a barometer that is being shaken, the scientific mind will not conclude from this that the vacuum of Torricelli *contained* latent fire.

The substantialization of fire easily reconciles its contradictory characteristics: fire can be quick and rapid in its dispersed forms; deep and lasting in its concentrated forms. It will only be necessary to invoke *substantial concentration* in order to account for its most varied aspects. For Carra, an author often quoted at the end of the eighteenth century:[6]

In straw and paper, the phlogiston component is very rare, whereas it is abundant in coal. The first two substances nevertheless flame up at the first approach of fire, whereas the latter takes a long time to burn. One can explain this difference in effect only by recognizing that the phlogiston component of straw and of paper, although rarer than that of coal, is in them less concentrated, more disseminated, and consequently more liable to a quick development.

Thus an insignificant experiment like that of a piece of paper being quickly set on fire is explained in its intensity by the degree of substantial concentration of the phlogiston. We must stress here this need to explain the *details* of a first experience. This need for minute explanation is quite symptomatic in non-scientific minds, which claim to neglect nothing and to take into account all the aspects of the concrete experience. The *quickness* of a fire thus offers false problems: this quickness made such a great impression on our imagination in our childhood! The straw fire remains, for the unconscious, a characteristic fire.

Similarly in the work of Marat, a prescientific mind of little intellectual power, the connection of the first experience with the substantialist intuition is equally direct. In a pamphlet which is merely a précis of his *Physical Research into Fire* (*Recherches physiques sur le Feu*), he expresses himself as follows:[7]

Why does the igneous fluid attach itself only to inflammable substances?—by virtue of a particular affinity between its globules and the phlogiston with which these substances are saturated. This attraction is quite obvious. When, by blowing air through a blowpipe, we attempt to separate from the combustible material the flame which is devouring it, we notice that it does not yield without resistance, and that it soon recaptures the space that it has abandoned." Marat might have added, to complete the animistic image which dominates his unconscious: "Thus dogs return to the prey from which they have been driven off.

This very familiar experience does indeed give us a measure of the tenacity of fire in holding fast to what it is consuming. We need only to try to extinguish a recalcitrant candle from a little distance away, or to blow out a flaming punch bowl, to gain a subjective measure of the resistance of fire. It is not so rude a resistance as that offered by inert objects to the touch. For this very reason it has all the more effect in determining the child to adopt an animistic theory of fire. In every circumstance the fire shows its ill will: it is hard to light; it is difficult to put out. The stuff is capricious; therefore fire is a person.

Of course this quickness and this tenacity of fire are secondary characteristics which have been entirely reduced and explained by scientific knowledge. A healthy abstraction has led us to neglect them. Scientific abstraction is the cure for the unconscious. Once it forms the basis of our education, it brushes aside the objections that are found scattered over the details of experience.

But it is perhaps the idea that fire *feeds itself* like a living creature which is foremost in the opinions developed about fire by our unconscious. For a modern mind, to feed a fire has become a commonplace synonym for keeping it going; but words dominate us more than we think, and the old image will at times come back to the mind when the old word comes back to the lips.

It is not difficult to assemble a good number of texts in which the *food* of fire keeps its literal primary meaning. A seventeenth-century author recalls that[8]

The Egyptians said that it was a ravening, insatiable animal which devours everything that experiences birth and growth; and, after it has eaten well and gorged itself, it finally devours itself when there is nothing left to eat and feast upon; because, having both heat and movement, it cannot do without food and the air it requires to breathe.

Vigenère develops his whole book from this initial inspiration. He finds in the chemistry of fire all the characteristics of digestion. Thus for him, as for many other writers, smoke is an excrement of fire. Another author, about the same period, writes that[9] "the Persians, when they made sacrifices to fire, would present food to it on the altar while uttering this phrase . . . 'Eat and feast, O Fire, lord of all the world.' "

In the eighteenth century, Boerhaave still

> . . . finds it necessary to make clear through a long investigation what must be understood by the *aliments of fire* . . . If we give them this appellation in a restricted sense, it is because we believe that these substances really do serve as food for Fire, that through its action they are converted into the proper substance of elementary Fire and that they lay aside their own primitive nature to take on that of Fire; in this case we are assuming a fact which deserves to be examined with mature deliberation.[10]

And this is what Boerhaave proceeds to do in a great many pages in which he himself offers a feeble resistance to the animistic intuition he is seeking to reduce. We are never completely immune to the prejudice that we spend a great deal of time in attacking. At any rate, Boerhaave saves himself from the animistic prejudice only by fortifying the substantialist prejudice: in his doctrine, the *food* of fire is transformed into the *substance* of fire. By assimilation, the aliment becomes fire. This assimilation of substance is the negation of the spirit of Chemistry. Chemistry is able to study the way in which substances are combined, are mixed together and remain juxtaposed. Those are three defensible notions. But Chemistry cannot study how one substance *assimilates* another. When it accepts this concept of *assimilation*, the more or less learned form of the concept of *food*, it throws light on the obscure by means of the more obscure; or rather it imposes on the objective explanation the false knowledge gained from an internal experience of digestion.

We shall see how extensive are the unconscious values attached to the *food of fire* and how desirable it is to psychoanalyze what could be called the *Pantagruel complex* in a prescientific unconscious mind. It is, in fact, a prescientific principle that everything that burns must receive the *pabulum ignis*. Thus one of the most common notions in the cosmologies of the Middle Ages and of the prescientific period is that of food for the stars. In particular, it is often the function of the terrestrial exhalations to serve as food for the stars. These exhalations feed the comets. The comets feed the sun. Let us examine only a few texts selected from recent periods in order to demonstrate the persistence and the force of the myth of digestion in the explanation of material phenomena. Thus Robinet writes in 1766:[11]

It has been stated with a good deal of probability that the luminous globes feed on the exhalations that they draw from the opaque globes, and that the natural food of the latter is the flood of igneous particles that the former are continually sending to them; and that the spots of the Sun which seem to spread and darken every day are nothing but an accumulation of crude vapors of expanding volume that the Sun attracts unto itself; that these clouds of smoke that we think we see rising from its surface are really rushing towards this surface; and that in the end it will absorb such a great quantity of heterogeneous material that it will not only be enveloped and encrusted by it, as Descartes claimed, but will be totally penetrated by it. When this happens it will be extinguished, it will die, so to speak, by passing from the state of light, which is its life, to the state of opacity, which we may call a true death when speaking of the Sun. In a similar fashion the leech dies when it has slaked its thirst for blood.

As one can see, the digestive intuition is all powerful: for Robinet, the Sun King will die from overeating.

This principle of the feeding of the stars by fire is, moreover, quite clear when one accepts the idea still quite prevalent among eighteenth-century thinkers that "all the stars are created from one and the same celestial substance of subtle fire." [12] They consider that a fundamental analogy exists between the stars formed of rarefied celestial fire and the metallic sulphurs formed of crude terrestrial fire. They believe that they have thereby united the phenomena of earth and sky and have obtained a universal view of the world.

And so the ancient ideas continue down through the ages; they keep recurring, even in more or less learned reveries, with all their charge of original naiveté. A seventeenth-century author will, for example, usually combine the opinions of antiquity and the opinions of his own time: [13] "By reason of the fact that during the day the stars attract the vapors in order to feed upon them at night, Euripides has called night the nursing mother of the golden stars." Were it not for the myth of digestion, were it not for this entirely stomachal rhythm of the Greater Being that is the Universe, a Being who sleeps and eats, adjusting his diet to the day and to the night, many prescientific or poetic intuitions would be inexplicable.

It is particularly interesting from the point of view of a psychoanalysis of objective knowledge to see how an intuition loaded with affectivity like the intuition of fire will offer itself as an explanation for new phenomena. This took place at the time when prescientific thought was trying to explain the phenomena of electricity.

It is not difficult to prove that the electric fluid is nothing but fire, once one is content to be swayed by the spell of the substantialist intuition. Thus the abbé de Mangin is very quickly convinced: [14] "In the first place, it is in all the bituminous and sulphurous bodies such as glass and pitch that the electric substance is found, since thunder draws its electric matter from the bitumens and sulphurs attracted by the action of the sun." Thus very little more is needed to prove that glass contains fire and to place it in the category of sulphurs and pitches. So for the abbé de Mangin "the sulphurous odor that glass emits when it happens to break after being rubbed is the convincing proof that the bitumens and the oils are dominant within it." Should we also recall the old etymology, always active in the prescientific mind, which claimed that corrosive vitriol was vitreous oil (*l'huile de vitre*)?

The intuition of inwardness, of intimacy, so strongly connected with the substantialist intuition, appears in the following example with an ingenuity that is all the more striking, since it claims to explain well-defined, scientific phenomena. "It is especially within the oils, the bitumens, the gums, the resins that God has locked up fire, as if in so many boxes capable of containing it." Once one has assented to the metaphor of a substantial property locked in a *box,* one's style becomes charged with images. If the electric fire

could insinuate itself into the cells of the little balls of fire which fill the tissue of bodies which are in themselves electric; if it could untie this multitude of little pouches which have the power to contain this hidden, secret and internal fire and if it could unite itself to it; then these particles of fire, now set free, shaken, compressed, dispersed, reunited and violently agitated, would communicate to the electric fire an action, a force, a speed, an acceleration, a fury which would disunite, break, set ablaze and destroy the compound.

But since this is impossible, bodies like resin, which are electric in themselves, must keep the fire locked up in their little boxes; they cannot receive electricity by communication. Here, then, full of imagery and laden with verbiage, is the *prolix explanation* of the nature of bodies that are poor conductors. Moreover, this explanation, which amounts to the denial of any special nature, is quite curious. The necessity of the conclusion is not very apparent. It would seem that this conclusion merely came to interrupt a smoothly developing reverie which had been really only a matter of piling up synonyms.

The realization that electric sparks coming from the charged human body could set fire to brandy caused real amazement. Electrical fire was then a true fire! Winckler lays great stress on "such an extraordinary event." The reason for this amazement is that these people could not understand how such a fire, brilliant, warm, and capable of setting things on fire, could be contained, without the least discomfort, in the human body! A mind as precise and meticulous as Winckler's does not question in any way the substantialist postulate, and it is from this absence of philosophical criticism that the false problem will be created:[15] "A fluid cannot set fire to anything unless it contains particles of fire." Since fire *comes out* of the human body, it is because it was *contained* beforehand within the human body. Is it necessary to call attention to the ease with which this inference is accepted by a prescientific mind which is unsuspectingly following the seductive delusions we have exposed in the preceding chapters? The only mystery is that this fire ignites alcohol outside the human body, whereas it does not set fire to the tissues inside the body. This lack of logic in the realistic intuition of fire did not lead, however, to any reduction in the concept of the *reality of fire*. The realism of fire is one of the most indestructible of intuitions.

The *realization* of heat and fire is also very striking when carried out in connection with particular substances such as the vegetable substances. The fascination of the realistic delusion can then lead to strange beliefs and practices. Here is one from among a great many examples that could be taken from Bacon (*Sylva Sylvarum*, para. 456): "It is reported that mulberries will be fairer, and the trees more fruitful, if you bore the trunk of the tree through in several places, and thrust into the places bored wedges of some hot trees, as turpentine, mastic-tree, guaiacum, juniper, etc. The cause may be, for that adventive heat doth cheer up the native juice of the tree." This belief in the efficacy of *hot* substances is long lasting in certain minds, but usually it diminishes and is gradually reduced to metaphor or symbol. It is in such a fashion that crowns of laurel have lost their original meaning: they are now made of green paper, but here is an example in which they are given their full value:[16] "The branches of that tree which antiquity dedicated to the Sun in order to crown all the conquerors of the Earth, when shaken together give out fire, as do the bones of lions." The realist conclusion will, moreover, presently appear: "The laurel cures ulcers of the head, and removes facial blemishes." Under the crown how radiant is a forehead! In our day, when all values are metaphors, laurel crowns cure nothing more than cases of ulcerated pride.

We are inclined to excuse all these naive beliefs, because we now interpret them only in their metaphorical translation. We forget that they corresponded to psychological realities. Now it often happens that metaphors have not completely lost their *reality*, their *concreteness*. There is still a trace of concreteness in certain soundly abstract definitions. A psychoanalysis of objective knowledge must retrace and complete this process of *de-realization*. What gives us a just measure of the errors concerning fire is the fact that they are still, perhaps more than any other type of error, attached to concrete affirmations, to unquestioned inner experiences.

Some very special characteristics, which should be the object of a special study, are thus explained by a mere reference to an inner fire. Such is the case for

> . . . the extraordinary vigor that we observe in certain plants . . . which contain within themselves a much more considerable quantity of this fire than certain others, which are, however, of the same species. Thus the sensitive plant (mimosa pudica) requires more of this fire than any other plant or natural thing, and I can then understand how it is that when some other body touches it, it must communicate to it a great part of its fire, which is its very life, so that it falls sick and lowers its leaves and branches until it has had time to recover its vigor by drawing in new fire from the air that surrounds it.

This inner fire that the sensitive plant gives forth until it is exhausted has for a psychoanalyst another name. It does not depend on any *objective* knowledge. One can see nothing which justifies *objectively* the claim that a limp sensitive plant is a plant exhausted of its *fire*. A psychoanalysis of objective knowledge must track down any scientific convictions which have not been formed from specifically objective experiments.

In all domains it is repeated without a shadow of proof that fire is the principle of life. The idea is of such antiquity that it is accepted as a matter of course. It seems that *in general* it is convincing, on condition that it is not applied to *any particular case*. The more precise the application, the more ridiculous it becomes. Thus a specialist on midwifery, after a long treatise on the growth of the embryo and the usefulness of the amniotic fluid, reaches the point where he professes that water, this liquid which is the carrier of all nourishment for the three kingdoms, must be animated by fire. At the end of his treatise can be seen a puerile example of the natural dialectic of fire and water:[17] "Vegetation is the work of that kind of avidity with which fire seeks to combine itself with water, which is its true moderator." This substantialist intuition of fire which seeks to *animate* water has such fascination that it induces our author "to go more deeply" into a scientific theory which has been too simply and too obviously based upon Archimedes' principle: "Will we never abandon the absurd opinion that water reduced to steam rises in the atmosphere because in this new state it is lighter than an equal volume of air?" For David, Archimedes' principle depends on a very inferior science of mechanics; on the contrary it is obvious that it is fire, the animating fluid, "never idle," which carries the water along and makes it rise. "Fire is perhaps this active principle, this second cause that has received all its energy from the Creator, and that Scripture has designated by these words: *et spiritus Dei ferebatur super aquas.*" Such is the flight of fancy embarked upon by a specialist in midwifery while meditating on amniotic fluids.

As a substance, fire is certainly among those to which the most values have been attributed and is hence the one which most distorts objective judgments. In many respects the value ascribed to fire equals that of gold. Gold, apart from its germinative value in the mutation of metals and its curative value in the prescientific pharmacopœia, has only its commercial value. Frequently it even happens that the alchemist will attribute a value to gold, because it is a receptacle of elementary fire: "The quintessence of gold is all fire." Moreover, in a general manner, fire, a veritable Proteus where the attribution of value is concerned, may pass from the most metaphysical values of principle to the most obvious utilitarian values. It is truly the fundamental active principle which sums up all the operations of nature. An eighteenth-century alchemist wrote:[18] "Fire . . . is nature, which does nothing in vain, which cannot err, and without which nothing is done." Let us note in passing that a Romantic would not speak any differently of passion. The slightest participation is sufficient; fire has only to set the seal of its presence to demonstrate its power: "Fire is always the least in quantity, as it is the first in quality." This powerful action of minute quantities is highly symptomatic. When it is postulated without any objective proofs, as is here the case, it is because the minute quantity under consideration is magnified by the will to power. We would like to be able to concentrate all chemical action into a handful of gunpowder, all hatred into one swift poison, an immense and unutterable love into a humble gift. In the unconscious of a prescientific mind, fire does perform actions of this kind: an atom of fire in certain cosmological dreams is sufficient to set a whole world ablaze.

The same author [Reynier] who criticizes simple images and who declares:[19] "We are no longer living in that century when the causticity and the action of certain solvents could be explained by the tenuity and the form of their molecules, that were supposed to be sharp wedges which penetrated bodies and separated their parts," writes a few pages further on: fire "is the element which gives animation to everything and to which everything owes its being; which, as the principle of life and death, of existence and non-existence, acts by itself and bears within itself the power to act." It would appear, then, that the critical spirit ceases to function when confronted by the inner power of fire; and that the explanation based on fire can penetrate to such depths that it can decide on the existence and the non-existence of things, and at the same time invalidate all the poor mechanistic explanations. At all times and in all fields the explanation by fire is a *rich* explanation. A psychoanalysis of objective knowledge must constantly denounce this claim to inner depth and richness. One is definitely justified in criticizing the ingenuousness of a fanciful atomism. Yet at least one must admit that it lends itself to an *objective* discussion, whereas the device of resorting to the power of an *imperceptible* fire, that is used to explain the causticity of certain solutions, quite precludes any possibility of objective verification.

The equation of fire and life forms the basis of the system of Paracelsus. For Paracelsus, fire is life, and whatever secretes fire truly bears the seed of life. Common mercury is precious in the eyes of the followers of Paracelsus, because it contains a very perfect fire and a celestial inner life, a statement that Boerhaave will also make.[20] It is this hidden fire that must be utilized for the curing of sickness and for procreation. Nicolas de Locques bases all the value he attributes to fire on its inwardness.[21] Fire is "internal or external; the external fire is mechanical, corrupting and destroying, the internal is spermatic, generative, ripening." In order to obtain the essence of fire one must go to its source, to its reserve, where it husbands its strength and concentrates itself, that is to say, to the mineral. Here, then, is the best justification for the method of the spagyrists (alchemists): "This life-producing celestial fire is very active in the animal which makes a greater dissipation of it than does the plant and the metal; that is why the philosopher is continually occupied with seeking means to replenish it; and seeing that it could not be long maintained by the fire of life which is in the animal and in plants, he has desired to seek it within the metal, where this fire is more fixed and incombustible, more withdrawn and more temperate in its action, leaving herbs for the followers of Galen to make into salads in which this blessed fire will be nothing but a mere spark."

In short, they believe so firmly in the universal empire of fire that they arrive at this hasty dialectical conclusion: since fire *is expended* in the animal, it is therefore *stored up* within the mineral. There it is hidden, inward, substantial, and hence all powerful. In the same way a retiring love is considered to be a faithful love.

Such a force of conviction in affirming the hidden powers of fire cannot come only from the external experience of well-being that is enjoyed in front of a bright fire. There must be added the great and wholly inward certainties of digestion—the pleasant comfort of hot soup, the wholesome warmth of the alcoholic stimulant. So long as a psychoanalysis has not been made of the man filled to repletion, we shall lack a knowledge of the primordial affective elements which would enable us to understand the psychology of realistic evidence. We have described elsewhere all that realistic chemistry owes to the myth of digestion. We could assemble innumerable quotations concerning the sensation of stomachal heat and the falsely objective inferences that have been attached to it. This sensation is often the perceptible principle of health and of sickness. With respect to sensations of slight pain, the books of the medical practitioners are particularly attentive to the "burning sensation," the "phlogoses," the desiccations which burn the stomach. Each author feels called upon to explain these burning sensations in terms of his system, for without an explanation of everything connected with the fundamental principle of vital heat the system would lose its entire value. Thus Hecquet explains the fire of digestion in the light of his theory of stomachal trituration by recalling that a wheel can catch fire by being rubbed along the ground. It is then the grinding of the foods by the stomach which produces the heat necessary "for their cooking." Hecquet is a scientist; he does not go so far as to believe certain anatomists who have "seen fire coming out of the stomachs of birds." [22] Nevertheless he gives this opinion some prominence, thereby demonstrating that the image of the man vomiting forth flames while dancing is a favorite image of the unconscious. The theory of the *inclemencies of the stomach* could lead to endless observations. One could seek out the origin of all the metaphors which have led to the classification of foods in accordance with their *heat,* their *coldness,* their *dry heat,* their *wet heat,* their *cooling virtue.* One would easily prove that the scientific study of alimentary values is distorted by prejudices formed by fleeting and trivial first impressions.

Thus we do not hesitate to claim a cœnesthetic origin for certain fundamental philosophical intuitions. In particular we believe that this inner, covered, preserved, possessed heat resulting from a well-digested meal leads men unconsciously to postulate the existence of a hidden and invisible fire in the interior of matter, or, as the alchemists would say, in the belly of the metal. The theory of this fire, immanent in matter, leads to a special form of materialism for which a word would have to be created, for it represents an important refinement of philosophical opinion intermediate between materialism and animism. This *calorism* corresponds to the materialization of a soul or to the animation of matter; it is a transitional form between matter and life. It is the mute awareness of the material assimilation performed by digestion, of the animalization of the inanimate.

By applying this myth of the digestion, we get a much better understanding of the meaning and the force of these words of the *Cosmopolite,* who causes mercury to say:[23] "I am all fire within; fire serves as my food, and it is my life." Another alchemist says in a way that is less picturesque, but which amounts to the same thing: "Fire is an element which is active at the center of each thing."[24] With what readiness a meaning is accorded to such an expression! After all, to say that a substance has an interior, a center, is hardly any less metaphorical than to say that it has a belly. To speak of a quality and a tendency amounts then to speaking of an appetite. To add, as does the alchemist, that this interior is a hearth, in which the indestructible fire-principle is smoldering, merely establishes metaphorical convergences centered on the certainties of digestion. It will take great efforts on the part of scientific objectivity to *detach* heat from the substances in which it appears in order to make of it an entirely transitive quality, an energy which in no case can be latent or hidden.

Not only does the interiorization of fire exalt its virtues, it also leads to the most categorical contradictions. In our opinion, this is the proof that we are here dealing not with *objective* properties but rather with psychological values. Man is perhaps the first natural object in which nature has tried to contradict itself. It is for this reason, moreover, that human activity is in the process of changing the face of the planet. But in this short monograph let us consider only the contradictions and falsehoods concerning fire. Thanks to this process of interiorization, writers end by speaking of an *incombustible fire.* After having worked over a piece of sulphur for a long time, Joachim Poleman writes:[25]

Just as this sulphur was naturally a burning fire and a dazzling light on the surface, now it is no longer external, but internal and incombustible; it is no longer a fire burning externally, but is burning internally; and just as before it would burn anything that was combustible, so now through its power it burns the invisible maladies, and, whereas sulphurs before they were baked would shine externally, they now no longer shine except in maladies or in spirits of darkness, which are none other than the spirits or properties of the shadowy bed of death . . . and the fire transmutes these spirits of darkness into good spirits such as they were when the man was in good health.

When one reads pages like these, one must ask oneself from what aspect they are clear and from what aspect they are obscure. Now this page of Poleman is certainly obscure from the objective point of view: a scientific mind conversant with chemistry and medicine will experience difficulty in giving a name to the experiences mentioned. On the other hand, from the subjective point of view, when one has made an effort to acquire the appropriate tools of psychoanalysis, when one has in particular isolated the complex of the sentiment of possession and the complex of the impressions of inner fire, then the pages become clear. This is then the proof that it has a subjective coherence and not an objective cohesion. This determination of the axis of explanation, whether it should be subjective or objective, appears to us to be the first diagnosis required for a psychoanalysis of knowledge. If, in a particular field of knowledge, the sum of personal convictions exceeds the sum of the items of knowledge that can be stated explicitly, taught, and proven, then a psychoanalysis is indispensable. The psychology of the scientist must tend towards a psychology that is clearly normative; the scientist must resist *personalizing his knowledge;* correlatively he must endeavor to *socialize his convictions.*

The best proof that physiological impressions of heat have been reified in prescientific knowledge is that inner heat has supplied references to determine *kinds of* heat that no modern experimenter would attempt to distinguish. In other words, the human body suggests *points of fire* to which the alchemical Artists endeavor to give concrete form. According to one of them,[26]

> The philosophers distinguish heat according to the difference in animal heat and divide it into three or four species: a digesting heat similar to that of the stomach, a generating heat like that of the uterus, a coagulating heat similar to that which makes the sperm, and a lactifying heat like that of the breasts . . . The stomachal heat is putrefying when digesting in the stomach, alimentary when generating in the womb, inspissative when decocting in the kidneys, the liver, the breasts and all else.

Thus the sensation of inner heat, with its thousand subjective nuances, is translated directly into a *science of adjectives,* as is always the case for a science hampered by the obstacles of substantialism and animism.

This reference to the human body will persist for a long time, even when the scientific attitude is quite well developed. When scientists wished to make the first thermometers, their first idea was to take the temperature of the human body as one of the fixed points to be used in graduating these instruments. Now we see the objective reversal that contemporary medicine has effected in determining the temperature of the body by comparison with physical phenomena. Popular knowledge, even in fairly accurate tests, works from the opposite point of view.

But "this benign heat, which foments our life," as a doctor describes it at the end of the eighteenth century, is still more symptomatic when it is considered, in its dispersion or in its synthesis, with no precise localization, as being the total realization of life. The muffled life force is really a dispersed heat. It is this vital fire which forms the basis for the idea of hidden fire, of invisible fire, of fire without flame.

When this idea becomes common, then scientific reveries can be given free rein. Now that the igneous principle has been deprived of its perceptible quality, now that fire is no longer the yellow flame, the red coal, now that it has become invisible, it can take on the most varied properties, the most diverse qualificatives. If we take *aqua fortis*, for example, we see that it consumes bronze and iron. Its hidden fire, its fire without heat, burns the metal without leaving any trace, like a well-planned crime. Thus this *simple but hidden* action, laden with unconscious reveries, will be covered over with adjectives in accordance with the rule of the unconscious: the less we know about something the more names we give it. To describe the fire of nitric acid (or *aqua fortis*), Trévisan[27] says that its hidden fire is "subtle, vaporous, digesting, continual, encompassing, airy, clear and pure, confined, non-flowing, corrupting, penetrating and sharp." Obviously these adjectives are not describing an object, they are revealing a feeling, probably an urge to destroy.

The burn caused by a liquid astonishes all minds. How many times have I seen my pupils amazed at the calcination of a cork through the action of sulphuric acid. In spite of my instructions—or, psychoanalytically speaking, because of my instructions—the blouses of the young experimenters suffered particularly from the acids. Through our thoughts we multiply the power of the acid. Psychoanalytically, the will to destroy is a coefficient of the destructive property recognized in the acid. In fact, *to think of a power means not only to use it, but above all to abuse it.* Were it not for this desire to misuse it, the consciousness of power would not be clearly felt. An anonymous Italian author, at the end of the seventeenth century, wonders at the inner power of heat that is found "in nitric acids and similar spirits which burn as strongly as fire even in winter, and with such effect that one would think them capable of destroying all of Nature and reducing it to nothingness . . ." It is perhaps interesting to compare this highly personal nihilism of an old Italian author with the following newspaper item (Rome, March 4, 1937): Gabriel d'Annunzio communicates a message which ends with the following Sibylline phrases: "From now on I am old and sick and that is why I am hastening my end. I have been forbidden to die in capturing Ragusa by assault. Disdaining to die quietly in bed, I shall try my last invention." And the newspaper explains what this invention consists of. "The poet has decided, when he feels the hour of death approaching, to plunge into a bath which will immediately cause death and instantly destroy the tissues of his body. It is the poet himself who discovered the formula for this liquid." In this way, then, does our scientific and philosophic reverie work: it accentuates all forces; it seeks the absolute in life as in death. Since we must disappear, since the instinct for death will impose itself one day on the most exuberant life, let us disappear and die completely. Let us destroy the fire of our life by a superfire, by a superhuman superfire without flame or ashes, which will bring extinction to the very heart of the being. When the fire devours itself, when the power turns against itself, it seems as if the whole being is made complete at the instant of its final ruin and that the intensity of the destruction is the supreme proof, the clearest proof, of its existence. This contradiction, at the very root of the intuition of being, favors endless transformations of value.

When prescientific thought has found a concept like that of latent fire, from which the predominant empirical characteristic has been effaced, it becomes strangely adaptable: it seems that, henceforth, it has the right to contradict itself openly and scientifically. Contradiction, which is the law of the unconscious, filters into prescientific knowledge. Let us now examine this contradiction in its crude form in the work of an author who professed to have a critical mind. For Reynier, as for Madame du Châtelet, fire is the principle of expansion. It is through expansion that it can be objectively measured. But this does not prevent Reynier from supposing that fire is the power which *contracts*, which *constricts*. It is to fire, he says,[28] that all bodies "owe the cohesion of their principles; without it, they would be incoherent," for "as soon as fire enters into a chemical combination, it contracts into a space infinitely smaller than that which it previously occupied." Thus fire is as much a principle of contraction as a principle of expansion; it disperses and it coheres. Moreover, this theory, put forward in 1787 by an author who wished to avoid any appearance of erudition, has a long history. The alchemists had already stated: "Heat is a quality which separates heterogeneous things and fuses homogeneous things." Since there was no contact between the authors quoted, it can be seen that we are in fact dealing with one of those subjectively natural intuitions which wrongly reconcile opposites.

We have taken this contradiction as an example because it concerns a geometrical property. It should then have been particularly intolerable. But if we were to take into account the more hidden contradictions that are connected with vaguer qualities, we would soon be convinced that this geometrical contradiction, like all the others, depends less on the *physics of fire* than on the psychology of fire. We are going to emphasize these contradictions in order to show that contradiction is, for the unconscious, more than a tolerance; it is really a need. It is, indeed, through contradiction that we most easily achieve originality, and originality is one of the dominant claims of the unconscious. When it is directed towards objective knowledge, this need for originality *over-estimates* the importance of the phenomenon, *materializes* slight differences, *ascribes causes* to accidents, just in the same way in which the novelist imagines a hero endowed with an unlikely number of special qualities and portrays a wilful character through a series of inconsistent actions. Thus for Nicolas de Locques,[29] "this celestial heat, this life-giving fire, is confined and dull in a dry substance, is much expanded in a wet substance, is very active in a hot substance and is congealed and mortified in a cold substance." Thus these writers prefer to say that fire is congealed within a cold substance rather than to accept the fact that it disappears. Contradictions are piled up in order to preserve for fire its full value.

But let us study a little more closely an author who has been credited by men of letters with the reputation of a scientist. Let us take the book of the Marquise du Châtelet. In the opening pages the reader is plunged into the middle of the drama: fire is a mystery and yet it is familiar! "It continually eludes our comprehension, although it is within ourselves." There is, then, an *inwardness* of fire, the function of which will be to contradict the *appearances* of fire. One is always different from what one allows others to see. And so Mme du Châtelet states explicitly that light and heat are *modes* and not *properties* of fire. With these metaphysical distinctions we are far removed from the pre-positive mentality that writers grant too indiscriminately to the experimenters of the eighteenth century. Mme du Châtelet then undertakes a series of experiments to separate that which shines from that which heats. She recalls that the rays of the Moon do not transmit any heat; even when concentrated in the focus of a lens they do not burn. The Moon is cold. These few reflections are sufficient to justify this strange proposition: "Heat is not essential to elementary Fire." By the fourth page of her dissertation, Mme du Châtelet has already displayed a profound and original mind by the mere fact of this single contradiction. As she says, she looks on Nature "with a different eye than the common herd." A few rudimentary experiments or simple observations are, however, sufficient for her to decide that fire, far from being heavy, as certain chemists claim, has a tendency to rise. Immediately these questionable observations lead her to formulate certain metaphysical principles.

Fire is then the perpetual antagonist of gravity, far from being subject to it; thus everything in Nature is in perpetual oscillation of expansion and contraction through the action of Fire upon bodies and through the reaction of the bodies, which oppose the action of fire through their weight and the cohesion of their parts . . . To insist that fire has weight is to destroy nature; indeed it removes from nature its most essential property, that which makes it one of the main instruments of the Creator.

Is it necessary to point out the disproportion between the experiments and the conclusions? In any case the ease with which a counter-law has been found to contradict the law of gravity appears to us to be quite symptomatic of an activity of the unconscious. The unconscious is the builder of massive dialectical arguments, which are so frequent in insincere discussions and so different from the clear and logical dialectics that are based on an explicit alternative. In one irregular detail the unconscious finds a pretext to formulate an opposing general law: a physics of the unconscious is always a physics of the exception.

Alcohol: *The Water That Flames*

Punch: *The Hoffmann Complex*

Spontaneous Combustions

One of the most obvious phenomenological contradictions was brought about by the discovery of alcohol—a triumph of the thaumaturgical activity of human thought. Brandy, or eau-de-vie, is also eau de feu or fire-water. It is a water which burns the tongue and flames up at the slightest spark. It does not limit itself to dissolving and destroying as does *aqua fortis*. It disappears with what it burns. It is the communion of life and of fire. Alcohol is also an *immediate* food which quickly warms the cockles of the heart: in comparison with alcohol, even meats are *slow acting*. Alcohol, therefore, has been attributed many obvious substantialist values. It, too, reveals its action in small quantities: it is more concentrated than the most exquisite of consommés. It conforms to the rule of desire for realistic possession: to hold a great power within a small volume.

Since brandy burns before our entranced eyes, since, from the pit of the stomach, it radiates heat to the whole person, it affords proof of the convergence of inner experience and objective experiment. This double phenomenology prepares *complexes* that a psychoanalysis of objective knowledge will be obliged to eliminate in order to rediscover a true freedom of experiment. Among these complexes there is one which is quite special and quite powerful; it is the one which, so to speak, closes the circle; when the flame has run across the alcohol, when the fire has left its mark and sign, when the primitive fire-water has become clearly enriched with shining, burning flames, then we drink it. Only brandy, of all the substances in the world, is so close to being of the same substance as fire.

In my youth, at the time of the great winter festivals, they used to prepare a *brûlot* (brandy burnt with sugar). My father would pour into a wide dish some marc-brandy produced from our own vineyard. In the center he would place pieces of broken sugar, the biggest ones in the sugar bowl. As soon as the match touched the tip of the sugar, a blue flame would run down to the surface of the alcohol with a little hiss. My mother would extinguish the hanging lamp. It was the hour of mystery, a time when a note of seriousness was introduced into the festivity. Familiar faces, which suddenly seemed strange in their ghastly paleness, were grouped about the round table. From time to time the sugar would sputter before its pyramid collapsed; a few yellow fringes would sparkle at the edges of the long pale flames. If the flames wavered and flickered, father would stir at the *brûlot* with an iron spoon. The spoon would come out sheathed in fire like an instrument of the devil. Then we would "theorize": to blow out the flames too late would make the *brûlot* too sweet; to put them out too soon would mean concentrating less fire and consequently diminishing the beneficent action of the *brûlot* against influenza. One of the watchers would tell of a *brûlot* that burned down to the last drop. Another would tell about the fire at the distillery when the barrels of rum "exploded like barrels of gunpowder," an explosion at which no one was ever present. At all costs we were bent on finding an objective and a general meaning for this exceptional phenomenon . . . Finally the *brûlot* would be in my glass: hot and sticky, truly an essence. And so how well I understand Vigenère when, in a rather affected manner, he speaks of the *brûlot* as "a little experiment . . . quite pleasant and exceptional." How well, too, I understand Boerhaave when he writes: "What seemed to me most agreeable in this experiment is that the flame called forth by the match at a place some distance from this bowl . . . will leap across and light the alcohol which is in this same bowl." Yes, this is the true mobile fire, the fire which plays over the surface of the being, which plays with its own substance, entirely liberated from its own substance, liberated from itself. It is the will-o'the-wisp domesticated, the devil's fire displayed in the center of the family circle. When, after such a spectacle, we savored the delightful taste of the drink, we were left with unforgettable memories of the occasion. Between the entranced eye and the comfortably-glowing stomach was established a Baudelairien correspondence that was all the stronger since it was all the more materialized. For the drinker of the *brûlot* how poor and cold and *obscure* is the experience of a drinker of hot tea!

If one has not had a personal experience of this hot sugared alcohol that has been born of flame at some joyful midnight festivity, one has little understanding of the romantic value of punch; one is deprived of a diagnostic method of studying certain *phantasmagorical poems*. For example, one of the most characteristic traits of the work of Hoffmann, the teller of fantastic tales, is the importance given to the phenomena of fire. A poetry of the flame runs through his entire work. Moreover, the punch complex is here so much in evidence that it could be called the Hoffmann complex. A superficial examination might lead one to conclude that the punch is a pretext for telling the stories and is the mere accompaniment of a festive evening. For example, one of the finest tales, *The Song of Antonia*, is related one winter's evening "around a table on which was flaming a great bowl full of the punch of friendship," but this invitation to the realm of the fantastic is only a prelude to the story; it is not an integral part of it. Although it is striking that such a moving tale should thus be placed under the sign of fire, in other cases the sign is really incorporated into the story. The loves of Phosphorus and the Lily illustrate the poetry of fire (third evening):

". . . desire, which is developing a beneficent heat throughout your whole being, will soon plunge into your heart a thousand sharp darts;

for . . . the supreme pleasure that is being kindled by this spark I am placing within you is the hopeless grief that will make you perish only to germinate again in a different form. This spark is thought!" "Alas!" sighed the flower in a plaintive tone, "Since such an ardor now enflames me, can I not be yours?"

In the same story when the witchcraft, which was to have brought back the student Anselme to the poor Veronica, is completed, there is nothing left "but a light flame rising from the spirits of wine which burn in the bottom of the cauldron." Later in the story the salamander, Lindhorst, goes in and out of the bowl of punch; the flames in turn absorb him and reveal him. The battle between the witch and the salamander is a battle of flames; the snakes come out of the tureen filled with punch. Madness and intoxication, reason and enjoyment are constantly presented in combination. From time to time there appears in the stories a worthy bourgeois who would like to "understand" and who says to the student:

"How did this cursed punch manage to go to our heads and cause us to commit a thousand follies?" These were the words of Professor Paulmann when on the following morning he entered the room that was still strewn with broken mugs, in the midst of which the unfortunate periwig, reduced to its primary elements, was floating about, dissolved in an ocean of punch.

Thus the rationalized explanation, the bourgeois explanation, the explanation through a confession of drunkenness, is brought in to moderate the phantasmagorical visions, so that the tale appears as being half rational, half dream, as partly subjective experience and partly objective perception, at once plausible in its cause and unreal in its effect.

M. Sucher in his research into *The Sources of the Marvellous Element in the Work of Hoffmann* (*Les sources du merveilleux chez Hoffmann*), makes no mention of the experiences of alcohol; he does note, however, in passing: "As for Hoffmann, he saw the salamanders only in the flames of the punch bowl."

But he does not draw the conclusion which appears to us to be self-evident. If, in the first place, Hoffmann did not see the salamanders except in the flaming punch on a winter's evening when ghosts make their appearance at the height of the festivities in order to cause men's hearts to tremble; if, in the second place, it is obvious that the fire demons play a prime role in the reverie of Hoffmann, then it must be admitted that it is the paradoxical flame of the alcohol which is the prime inspiration, and that a whole section of his work becomes clear when studied in this light. It seems to us, then, that M. Sucher, in his subtle, intelligent study, has deprived himself of an important element of explanation. One should not be too ready to turn to rational constructions in seeking to understand an original literary genius. The unconscious, too, is a source of originality. Specifically, the alcoholic unconscious is a profound reality. One is mistaken if one imagines that alcohol simply stimulates our mental potentialities. In fact it creates these potentialities. It incorporates itself, so to speak, with that which is striving to express itself. It appears evident that alcohol is a creator of language. It enriches the vocabulary and frees the syntax. In point of fact, to return to the problem of fire, psychiatry has recognized the frequency of dreams about fire in cases of alcoholic delirium; it has shown that Lilliputian hallucinations are brought about by the excitation of alcohol. Now the reverie which leads to the miniature also leads to depth and stability: it is the reverie which in the final analysis best prepares us for engaging in rational thought. Bacchus is a beneficent god; by causing our reason to wander he prevents the anchylosis of logic and prepares the way for rational inventiveness.

Equally symptomatic is this page of Jean-Paul Richter, written, in what is already a Hoffmann-like tonality, on a New Year's Eve when, gathered around the pale flame of a punch bowl, the poet and four of his friends suddenly resolved to *look at one another as if they were already dead:*

It was as if the hand of death had squeezed the blood out of all the faces; the lips became bloodless, the hands white and elongated;

the room became a burial vault . . . In the moonlight a silent wind was tearing and whipping at the clouds, and in the places where the clouds left gaps in the open sky one could make out the darkness extending even beyond the stars. All was silent; the dying year seemed to struggle, utter its last sigh, and sink into the tombs of the past. O Angel of Time, you who have counted the sighs and the tears of mankind, forget them or hide them away! Who could bear the thought of their infinite number? [1]

How little it takes to make the reverie veer in one direction or another! It is a holiday; the poet, glass in hand, is drinking with his joyous companions; but a livid glow coming from the *brûlot* gives a dismal tone to even the most youthful songs; suddenly the pessimism induced by the ephemeral fire leads to a change in the reverie, the dying flame symbolizes the departing year, and time, the source of all woes, weighs down heavily upon their hearts. If it is again objected that the punch of Jean-Paul is but a pretext for a phantasmagorical idealism, scarcely any more material than the magic idealism of Novalis, it will have to be admitted that this pretext finds a ready development in the unconscious mind of the reader. In our opinion, this is proof that contemplation of objects to which many values are attached can release reveries whose development is as regular and as inevitable as that of sense-experiences.

Less profound souls will give off more artificial sonorities, but the fundamental theme will always ring through. O'Neddy sings in the *First Night* of *Fire and Flame* (*Première nuit* de *Feu et Flamme*):

In the center of the room, around an iron bowl
In size a worthy rival of the cups of hell,
Wherein a lovely punch shines with prismatic flames,
And rolls its waves along like some great sulphurous lake,

And the only ray of light in all the gloomy loft
Comes from the sheaf of flame, a spirituous mirage.
What a pure Ossianism is there in the crowning
Of heads whose dull white brows . . .

While this is bad poetry, these lines bring together all the traditions attached to the *brûlot* and illustrate quite clearly, in their poetic poverty, the Hoffmann complex, which lays a veneer of learned thought over naive impressions. For the poet, sulphur and phosphorus feed the prism of the flames; hell is present in this impure festivity. If the *values* of the reverie before the fire were missing from these pages, they would not have enough poetic *value* to make them worth reading. The reader's unconscious makes up for the inadequacy of the poet's unconscious. The stanzas of O'Neddy are of interest only because of the "Ossianism" of the flame from the punch. For us they are the evocation of a whole period when the romantic Jeunes-France would gather around the Bol de Punch,[2] when Bohemian existence was illuminated, as Henry Murger says, by the "*brûlots* of passion."

No doubt this period seems dead and gone. Nowadays punch and the *brûlot* have lost their psychological values. Teetotalism, with all its censorious slogans, has forbidden such experiences. It is nonetheless true, in my opinion, that a whole area of phantasmagorical literature is dependent upon the poetic excitation of alcohol. The precise and concrete bases must not be forgotten, if we wish to understand the psychological meaning of literary constructions. It would be profitable to examine the leading themes one by one in their precise details without submerging them too quickly in general surveys. If our present work serves any useful purpose, it should suggest a classification of objective themes which would prepare the way for a classification of poetic temperaments. We have not yet been able to perfect an over-all doctrine, but it seems quite clear to us that there is some relation between the doctrine of the four physical elements and the doctrine of the four temperaments. In any case, the four categories of souls in whose dreams fire, water, air, or earth predominate, show themselves to be markedly different. Fire and water, particularly, remain enemies even in reverie, and the person who listens to the sound of the stream can scarcely comprehend the person who hears the song of the flames: they do not speak the same language.

By developing in all its general implications this Physics, or this Chemistry of reverie, one would easily arrive at a tetravalent doctrine of poetic temperaments. Indeed, the tetravalence of reverie is as clear and as productive as the chemical tetravalence of carbon. Reverie has four domains, four points from which it soars into infinite space. To surprise the secret of a true poet, of a sincere poet, of a poet who is faithful to his original language and is deaf to the discordant echoes of sensuous eclecticism, which would like to play on all the senses, one word is sufficient: "Tell me what your favorite phantom is. Is it the gnome, the salamander, the sylph or the undine?" Now—and I wonder if this has been noticed—all these chimerical beings are formed from and sustained by a unique substance: the gnome, terrestrial and condensed, lives in the fissure of the rock, guardian of the mineral and the gold, and stuffs himself with the most compact substances; the salamander, composed all of fire, is consumed in its own flame; the water nymph or undine glides noiselessly across the pond and feeds on her own reflection; the sylph for whom the least substance is a burden, who is frightened away by the tiniest drop of alcohol, who would even perhaps be angry with a smoker who might "contaminate her element" (Hoffmann), rises effortlessly into the blue sky, happy in her anorexia.

Such a classification of poetic inspirations should not, however, be attached to a more or less materialistic hypothesis which would claim to discover a predominant material element in human flesh. We are not dealing here with matter, but with orientation. It is not a question of being rooted in a particular substance, but of tendencies, of poetic exaltation. Now it is the primitive images which orient psychological tendencies; these were the sights and impressions which suddenly aroused an interest in what is normally devoid of interest, which gave an *interest to the object*. It is upon this image to which new values have been attributed that the whole imagination has converged; and thus it is that through a narrow gate the imagination, as Armand Petitjean has said, "transcends us and brings us face to face with the world." The total *conversion* of the imagination that Armand

Petitjean has analyzed with an astonishing lucidity[3] is prepared for, as it were, by this preliminary translation of the block of images into the language of one preferred image. If we were correct in our theory of this imaginative polarization, then it would become more evident why two minds, apparently congeneric like those of Hoffmann and Edgar Allan Poe, are ultimately revealed to be profoundly different. Both were given powerful aid in their superhuman and inhuman work of genius by the power of alcohol. But the alcoholism of Hoffmann appears very different from that of Edgar Allan Poe. The alcohol of Hoffmann is the alcohol which flames up; it is marked by the wholly qualitative and masculine sign of fire. The alcohol of Poe is the alcohol that submerges and brings forgetfulness and death; it is marked by the wholly quantitative and feminine sign of water. The genius of Edgar Allan Poe is associated with the sleeping waters, the dead waters, with the tarn which reflects the *House of Usher*. He hears "the distant murmur through the turbulent water" following the "opiate vapor, dewy, dim," which softly drips "drop by drop . . . into the universal valley," while "the lake a conscious slumber seems to take." (*The Sleeper*) For him the mountains and the cities "topple evermore into seas without a shore." It is near the swamps, the dismal tarns and pools "Where dwell the Ghouls, By each spot the most unholy, In each nook most melancholy," that he again finds the "Sheeted Memories of the Past, Shrouded forms that start and sigh As they pass the wanderer by." (*Dreamland*) If he thinks of a volcano it is to see it flowing like the water of rivers: "my heart was volcanic as the scoriac rivers that flow." Thus the element to which his imagination has become polarized is water or lifeless earth on which no flower grows; it is not fire. One will also be convinced of this psychoanalytically in reading the admirable work of Mme Marie Bonaparte.[4] Here it will be seen that the fire symbol rarely intervenes except to call up the opposite element, water; that the flame symbol operates only in a repellent mode, as a crudely sexual image, against which the tocsin is rung. The symbolism of the fireplace here appears as the symbolism of a cold vagina into which the murderers shove and wall up their victim. Edgar Poe was truly "without hearth or home," the child of travelling actors, the child frightened when very young by the vision of a mother still young and smiling stretched out in the sleep of death. Alcohol itself did not warm him, comfort him, or make him gay! Poe never danced around a blazing punch bowl like a human flame, while holding hands with joyful companions. None of the complexes which are formed in the love of fire came to sustain and inspire him. Water alone gave him his horizon, his infinite, the unfathomable depths of his sorrow, and one would have to write an altogether different book to elucidate the poetry of sails and of glimmering lights, the poetry of the vague fear which makes us shudder by causing to resound within us the moanings of the Night.

In the preceding pages we have seen the poetic mind acting in complete obedience to the charm of a favorite image; we have seen it magnify all the possibilities, think of the great as modelled on the small, of the general as modelled on the vivid image, of power modelled on an ephemeral force, and of hell modelled on the *brûlot*. We are now going to show that the prescientific mind, in its original impulse, functions in almost the same way and that it, too, magnifies power in a fashion that is mistakenly overvalued by the unconscious. We shall see alcohol depicted as having such manifestly horrible effects that it will not be difficult for us to read the *observers' will to moralize* in the phenomena that are described. Thus, whereas the anti-alcohol movement in the nineteenth century developed along evolutionist lines, by charging the drinker with being responsible for all the defects of his race, we shall see teetotalism develop in the eighteenth century along the then predominant substantialist line. The will to condemn others always employs the weapon closest to hand. In a more general way, apart from the usual moralizing lesson, we shall have another example of the inertia of the obstacles of substantialism and animism at the threshold of objective knowledge.

Since alcohol is eminently combustible, it is easy to imagine that persons who indulge in spirituous liquors become, as it were, *impregnated* with inflammable substances. We do not seek to find out if the assimilation of alcohol transforms it. The Harpagon complex, which dominates culture as it does every material occupation, makes us think that we lose nothing of what we absorb and that all precious substances are carefully stored away: fat produces fat; the phosphates produce bones; blood gives blood; alcohol gives alcohol. In particular, the unconscious cannot admit that a quality as characteristic and as marvellous as inflammability can totally disappear. This, then, is the conclusion: whoever drinks alcohol may burn like alcohol. The substantialist conviction is so strong that the *facts*, which undoubtedly could be accounted for by various more normal explanations, will impose themselves on the credulity of the public throughout the course of the eighteenth century. Here are some of these facts, quoted as being quite authentic by Socquet, an author of some repute, in his *Essay on Heat* (*Essai sur le Calorique*) published in 1801. All these examples are taken, we should note in passing, from the "Age of Enlightenment."

We read in the public records of Copenhagen, that in 1692 a woman of the lower classes, whose nourishment was derived almost solely from an immoderate use of spirituous liquors, was found one morning entirely consumed by fire except for the final joints of the fingers and the skull . . .

The *Annual Register* of London for 1763 (vol. XVIII, p. 78) reports the case of a woman aged fifty, much addicted to drunkenness, who, over a period of a year and a half, had drunk a pint of rum or brandy per day, and who was found almost entirely reduced to ashes, between her fireplace and her bed, while the bed clothes and other articles of furniture had suffered little damage; a fact which merits attention.

This final remark reveals quite clearly that the intuition is satisfied by this assumption of a wholly internal and substantial kind of combustion which in some way can recognize its preferred fuel.

We find in the *Systematic Encyclopedia* (*Encyclopédie méthodique*) (Article, *Pathological Anatomy of Man*) the story of a woman about fifty years of age who, by indulging in a constant abuse of spirituous liquors, was likewise burnt up in the space of a few hours." Vicq-d'Azyr, who cites this fact, far from disputing it, declares that there have been many other similar cases.

> The Transactions of the Royal Society of London offer an equally striking phenomenon . . . A sixty-year-old woman was found incinerated one morning after having, it is said, drunk heavily of spirituous liquors the preceding evening. The furniture had suffered little damage and the fire in the hearth was completely extinguished. This fact is attested to by a large number of eye witnesses . . .
>
> Le Cat, in a *Report on Spontaneous Fires* (*Mémoire sur les incendies spontanés*), cites several cases of human combustion of this type.

Others may be found in the *Essay on Human Combustions* (*Essai sur les Combustions humaines*) of Pierre-Aimé Lair.

Jean-Henri Cohausen, in a book printed in Amsterdam under the title of *Lumen novum Phosphoris accensum*, relates "that a gentleman at the time of Queen Bona Sforza, having drunk a large quantity of brandy, vomited flames and was consumed by them."

In the *Ephémérides* (almanac) of Germany one again reads that

> often in the northern countries, flames shoot up from the stomachs of those who drink freely of strong liquors. It was seventeen years ago, says the author, that three gentlemen of Courlande, whose names propriety forbids me to mention, having vied with one another in drinking strong liquor, two of these gentlemen died, burned and suffocated by a flame which came forth from their stomachs.

Jallabert, one of the authors most often cited as being conversant with the technicalities of electrical phenomena, was relying in 1749 on similar "facts" to explain the production of electrical fire by the human body. A woman suffering from rheumatism had rubbed her body for a long time with camphorated spirits of wine. She was found one morning reduced to ashes without there being any grounds for suspecting that either fire from heaven or common fire had played any part in this strange accident. "It can be attributed only to the fact that the most tenuous parts of the sulphurs of the body having been greatly agitated by the rubbing and mixed in with the most subtle particles of the camphorated spirits of wine are very apt to cause a fire." [5] Another author, Mortimer, gives this advice:[6] "I am very much of the opinion that it would be dangerous for persons accustomed to drinking a good deal of spirituous liquor or to using embrocations of camphorated spirits of wine to have themselves electrified."

These writers consider the substantial concentration of alcohol in the flesh to be so strong that they dare to speak of a *spontaneous combustion*, so that the drunkard does not even need a match to set himself on fire. In 1766 the Abbé Poncelet, an emulator of Buffon, will say: "Heat, as the principle of life, sets in motion and maintains the activity of the animal constitution, but when it is increased to the degree of fire it causes strange ravages. Have we not seen drunkards, whose bodies were superabundantly impregnated with burning spirits because of the habitual excessive drinking of strong liquor, who have suddenly caught fire of themselves and have been consumed by spontaneous combustions?" Thus burning due to alcoholism is only a particular case of an abnormal concentration of heat.

Certain authors go so far as to speak of deflagration. An ingenious distiller, author of a *Chemistry of Taste and Smell* (*Chimie du Goût et de l'Odorat*), points out in these terms the dangers of alcohol:[7] "Alcohol spares neither muscle, nor nerve, nor lymph, nor blood, which it inflames to such a point that it causes to perish by a surprising, instantaneous deflagration those who dare to carry excess to its final stage."

In the nineteenth century there are virtually no reports of cases of spontaneous combustion, the terrible punishment for alcoholism. They gradually become metaphorical and give way to ready jokes about the red faces of drunkards, about the rubicund nose that a match could set on fire. These jokes are, moreover, immediately understood, a fact which proves that prescientific thought lingers on for a long time in the spoken language. It also lingers on in literature. Balzac has the prudence to refer to it through the mouth of a shrew. In *Le Cousin Pons*, Mme Cibot, the (un)lovely oyster seller, says in her incorrect speech:[8] "That woman, you know, 'as 'ad no luck because of her man, who drank everything in sight and who died of a spontaneous *imbustion.*"

On the other hand Emile Zola, in one of his most "scientific" books, *Le Docteur Pascal*, gives a long account of the spontaneous combustion of a human being:[9]

Through the hole in the material, already as large as a five-franc piece, the naked thigh could be seen, a red thigh from which was coming forth a little blue flame. At first Félicité thought it was cloth, the underpants or the shirt, that was burning. But doubt was no longer permitted; she was indeed looking upon the bare flesh; and the little blue flame was escaping from this flesh, light and dancing like a flame flickering across the surface of a bowl of blazing spirits. It was scarcely any higher than the flame of a night lamp, was quiet and gentle and so unstable that the slightest breath of air caused it to move about.

Evidently what Zola is transporting into the realm of facts is his reverie before his punch bowl, his Hoffmann complex. Following this passage, the substantialist intuitions that we have illustrated in the preceding pages are displayed in all their ingenuousness: "Félicité understood that her uncle was catching fire there like a sponge soaked with brandy. He had been saturated for years with the strongest and most inflammable of brandies. Undoubtedly he would presently be aflame from head to foot." As can be seen, the living flesh has no thought of losing the glasses of proof spirits that have been absorbed in the previous years. It is more agreeable for us to imagine that alimentary assimilation is a careful concentration, an avaricious capitalization of the cherished substance.

The next day when Doctor Pascal comes to see uncle

Macquart, just as in the prescientific accounts we have cited, he finds no more than a handful of fine ashes in front of the chair, which has been scarcely blackened. Zola even somewhat overdoes it: "Nothing remained of him, not a bone, not a tooth, not a nail, nothing but this pile of grey dust that the draft of air from the doorway threatened to sweep away at any moment." And here finally we see appear the secret desire for an apotheosis through fire; Zola hears the call of the all-consuming funeral pyre, of the inner funeral pyre; the novelist indicates very clearly that the Empedocles complex is at work in his unconscious: uncle Macquart had then died "royally like the prince of drunkards, flaming up spontaneously and being consumed in the burning pyre of his own body . . . just imagine setting fire to oneself like a Saint John's fire!" Where did Zola see any bonfires of the summer solstice that could set themselves aflame as do the ardent passions? What better way is there to confess that the meaning of the objective metaphors has been reversed and that it is in the inner recesses of the unconscious that is found the inspiration for the burning flames which can, from within, consume a living body?

Such a story, entirely a product of the imagination, is particularly disturbing when it comes from the pen of a *naturalist* writer who used to say modestly, "I am only a scientist." It leads one to think that Zola built up his image of science on most naive reveries, and that his theories of heredity derive from the simple intuition of a past which has engraved itself on matter in a form that is no doubt as meanly substantialist, as flatly realistic, as the *concentration* of alcohol in a human body, of fire in a fevered heart.

Thus story-tellers, doctors, physicists, novelists, all of them dreamers, start off from the same images and pass on to the same thoughts. The Hoffmann complex binds them to an early image, to a memory of childhood. According to their temperament, in obedience to their personal "phantom," they enrich the subjective or objective aspect of the object they are contemplating. From the flames which emanate from the *brûlot* they fabricate men of fire or streams of substance. In all cases they *attribute values;* they call upon all their own passions to explain a shaft of flame. They put their whole heart into "communicating" with a spectacle which fills them with wonderment and which therefore deceives them.

CHAPTER SEVEN

Idealized Fire:

Fire and Purity

Max Scheler has shown the excessive elements to be found in the theory of *sublimation* as developed by classical psychoanalysis. This theory follows the same inspiration as the utilitarian doctrine upon which evolutionist explanations are based.

The moral science of the naturalists always confuses the kernel and the shell. When they see that men who aspire to saintliness must, in order that they may explain to themselves and to others all the ardor of their love for spiritual and divine things, resort to words of a language which is not made to express such rare things, and must employ images, analogies and comparisons borrowed from the sphere of a purely sensual love, then these naturalists do not fail to say: we are here dealing merely with a veiled sexual desire, that is masked or shrewdly sublimated.[1]

In a penetrating analysis, Scheler denounces this "feeding from the roots" theory, which would deny man any chance of an existence on a higher plane. Now, while it is true that poetic sublimation, particularly romantic sublimation, keeps contact with the life of the passions, we can, as it happens, discover in souls who struggle against their passions a sublimation of another type that we shall call *dialectical sublimation*, in order to distinguish it from the *continuous sublimation* which is the only one envisaged by classical psychoanalysis.

An objection will be made to this dialectical sublimation on the grounds that psychic energy is homogeneous, is limited, and cannot be detached from its normal biological function. It will be said that a radical transformation would leave a blank, a void, a disturbance, in the original sexual activities. Such a materialistic intuition seems to us to have been acquired from contact with the accumulation of *neurotic cases* upon which the classical psychoanalysis of the passions is based. In point of fact, in our own field of study, through the application of psychoanalytical methods to the activity of *objective knowledge*, we have arrived at the conclusion that *repression* is a normal activity, a useful activity, better, a joyful activity. There can be no scientific thought without repression. Repression is at the origin of concentrated, reflective and abstract thought. Every coherent thought is constructed on a system of sound, clear inhibitions. There is a *joy in accepting limitations* inherent in all joy of learning. It is insofar as it is joyful that a well-founded repression becomes dynamic and useful.

To justify repression, we propose then the inversion of the useful and the agreeable, by insisting on the supremacy of the agreeable over the necessary. In our opinion the truly anagogical cure does not consist of liberating the repressed tendencies, but of substituting for the unconscious repression a conscious repression, a constant will to self-correction. This transformation is very evident in the rectification of an objective or rational error. Before being subjected to the psychoanalysis of objective knowledge, a scientific error is implicated in a philosophical viewpoint; it resists any reduction; it persists, for example, in explaining phenomenal properties along substantialist lines in accordance with a realistic philosophy. After having been subjected to the psychoanalysis of objective knowledge, the error is recognized as such, but it remains as an object of good-natured polemic. What a deep joy there is in making confessions of *objective* errors! To admit that one has erred is to pay the most signal homage to the perspicacity of one's mind. By so doing we re-live our education, intensify it, illuminate it with converging rays of light. We also externalize, proclaim and teach it. Then is born pure intellectual enjoyment.

But how much more intense is this enjoyment when our objective knowledge is the objective knowledge of the *subjective*, when we discover in our own heart the human universal, when, after having honestly psychoanalyzed our study of self, we integrate the rules of morality with the laws of psychology! Then the fire which was consuming us suddenly enlightens us. The haphazard passion becomes the deliberate passion. Love becomes family; fire becomes hearth and home. This normalization, this socialization, this rationalization, are often, because of the awkwardness of the new forms of expression, considered to represent a cooling down of the passions. They arouse the ready mockery of the advocates of an anarchical, spontaneous love still fired by the primitive instincts. But for the man who spiritualizes his emotions, the resulting purification is of a strange sweetness, and the consciousness of purity pours forth a strange light. Purification alone can permit us to examine dialectically the fidelity of a great love without destroying it. Although it discards a heavy mass of substance and fire, purification contains more possibilities, and not less, than the natural impulse. Only a *purified love* permits a deepening of the affections. It individualizes them. The charm of novelty yields progressively to the knowledge of character. "Certainly," says Novalis,[2] "An unknown mistress possesses a unique charm. But the yearning for the unknown, the unexpected, is extremely dangerous and harmful." In the passion of love more than in anything else, the need for constancy must dominate the need for adventure.

But we cannot here develop at length this thesis of a dialectical sublimation which finds its joy in a clearly systematic repression. It is sufficient to have indicated the general idea. We shall now see how it functions in respect to the precise problem we are studying in this short book. The fact that this particular study could be carried out so easily will be a proof, moreover, that the problem of the knowledge of fire is a true problem of *psychological structure.* Our book will then appear as a specimen of a whole series of studies, mediating between subject and object, which could be undertaken to show the fundamental influence on the life of the mind of certain meditations aroused by objects.

If the psychological problem of fire lends itself so easily to an interpretation in terms of dialectical sublimation, it is because the properties of fire, as we have already so often remarked, appear to be charged with numerous contradictions.

In order to come at once to the essential point and to demonstrate the possibility of two centers of sublimation, let us study the dialectic of the purity and the impurity that have both been attributed to fire.

That fire should at times be the sign of sin and evil is easy to understand, if one will recall what we said about sexualized fire. Every struggle against the sexual impulses must then be symbolized by a struggle against fire. A great number of texts could easily be found in which the demoniac character of fire is either explicit or implicit. The literary descriptions of hell, the engravings and pictures representing the devil with his tongue of fire, would provide grounds for a very clear psychoanalysis.

Let us move then to the opposite pole and see how fire has managed to become a symbol of purity. To do this we must confine ourselves to properties that are distinctly phenomenal. That is the price to be paid for the method we have chosen for this book, in which we must base all our ideas on objective facts. In particular we shall not deal with the theological problem of purification by fire. To give a full account of that would require a very long study. It is sufficient to point out that the core of the problem lies in the *contact* of the metaphor and the reality: is the fire which will set the world ablaze at the Last Judgment, is the fire of Hell, the same or not the same as terrestrial fire? Texts are equally numerous in support of both views, for it is not an article of faith that the fire of Hell should be of the same nature as our fire. This diversity of opinion can, moreover, call attention to the enormous flowering of metaphors around the primary image of fire. All these flowery expressions used by theology to adorn "our brother, the fire," would merit patient classification. Since, however, we have made it our task to determine the *objective* roots of poetic and moral images, we must restrict ourselves to seeking the *perceptible bases* for the principle which claims that *fire purifies everything*.

One of the most important reasons for attributing to fire a value of this kind could probably be its power of *deodorization.* In any case this is one of the direct proofs of purification. The odor is a primitive quality which imperiously compels recognition either by its most insidious or by its most importunate presence. It truly violates our privacy. Fire is *all-purifying* because it suppresses nauseous odors. There again the *agreeable takes precedence over the useful*, and we cannot follow the interpretation of Frazer, who claims that cooked food gave more strength to the men of a tribe who, having won the secret of fire for cooking, were better able to digest the prepared food, and, being thereby made stronger, were able to impose their rule upon neighboring tribes. Above this real, materialized strength resulting from an easier digestive assimilation of food, there must be placed the imagined strength produced by the awareness of well-being, of inner satisfaction, and by the feeling of conscious pleasure. Cooked meat represents above all the overcoming of putrefaction. Together with the fermented drink it constitutes the principle of the banquet, that is to say the principle of primitive society.

By its deodorizing action fire seems to transmit one of the most mysterious, the most imprecise, and consequently the most striking of values. It is this perceptible value which forms the phenomenological basis for the idea of *substantive virtue.* A psychology of primitiveness must devote a good deal of attention to the olfactory psychism.

A second reason for the principle of purification by fire, a reason that is much more sophisticated and consequently much less efficacious from the psychological point of view, is that fire separates substances and destroys material impurities. In other words, that which has gone through the ordeal of fire has gained in homogeneity and hence in purity. The smelting and the forging of mineral ores have supplied a cluster of metaphors which all tend to attribute the same sort of value. Nevertheless the activities of smelting and forging remain exceptional experiences, scientific experiences, which have a great deal of influence on the reverie of the bookish man who acquaints himself with rare phenomena, but which have very little influence on the natural reverie which always returns to the primitive image.

Finally, in the same category as these fires of fusion, there should doubtless be placed the agricultural fire, that which purifies the fields. This purification is truly conceived as going deep into the earth. Not only does the fire destroy the useless weed, but it enriches the soil. In this connection we should perhaps recall the thoughts of Virgil, which are still present in the minds of our ploughmen:

> Often, too, it is good to set fire to a sterile field and to deliver the light stubble to the crackling flame; whether it is that the fire communicates to the soil a secret virtue and more abundant juices; whether it purifies it and dries up its superfluous humidity; whether it opens the subterranean pores and canals which carry the sap to the roots of the new plants; whether it hardens the soil, contracts the veins that are too open and closes up their entrance against excessive rains, against the burning rays of the sun, or against the glacial breath of Boreas.[3]

As always, under the multiplicity of explanations, which are often contradictory, there lies an unquestioned primitive value. But the value here attributed remains ambiguous: it unites the thought of suppressing an evil with the thought of producing a good. It is thus ideally suited to give us an understanding of the precise dialectic of objective purification.

Let us consider now the region in which fire is thought to be pure. This region, it seems, is at the extreme limit, at the point of the flame, where color gives way to an almost invisible vibration. Then fire is dematerialized; it loses its reality; it becomes pure spirit.

On the other hand the complete purification of the concept of fire is retarded by the fact that fire leaves ashes. The ashes are often thought of as true excretions. Thus Pierre Fabre believes that Alchemy, in the early days of humanity, was[4] "very powerful because of the power of its natural fire . . . so all things were seen to last longer than they do at present, since this natural fire is now much weakened by being attached to a great, enormous quantity of excrements that it cannot throw off and which cause it to be entirely extinguished in a great number of individuals." Hence we have the necessity of renewing the fire, of returning to the original fire, which is the pure fire.

Conversely, when the *impurity* of fire is suspected, these eighteenth-century writers appear determined to call attention to the residues of fire. Thus they consider that *the normal fire of the blood* is of a great purity; in the blood "resides that vivifying fire by which man exists; thus it is always the last thing to be corrupted; and when it comes to a state of corruption it does not do so until a few moments after death."[5] But fever is the mark of an impurity in the fire of the blood; it is the mark of an impure sulphur. So one must not be astonished that fever coats "the respiratory passages, and principally the tongue and the lips, with a black, burnt fuliginousness."[6] Here may be seen the power of explanation that a metaphor can have for a naive mind, when this metaphor is working upon an essential theme such as that of fire.

The same author led up to his theory of fevers by referring to the distinction between pure and impure fire as if it were an indisputable fact.

There are in nature two kinds of fire: the one which is made of a very pure sulphur, separated from all the earthly and crude parts, like that of spirits of wine, that of the lightning bolt, etc., and the other which is made from sulphurs that are crude and impure because they are mixed with earth and salts; such are the fires which are made from wood and bituminous substances. The hearth on which these substances are burnt seems to us to reveal this difference quite clearly; for the former fire leaves in it no perceptible substance that it has sloughed off, everything being consumed by combustion. But the fire of the latter order produces a considerable smoke as it burns and leaves in the chimney pipes a great quantity of soot . . . and of useless earth.

This commonplace observation is sufficient to make our doctor describe the impurity of a fevered blood as being dominated accidentally by *impure fire*. Another doctor also says: "It is a burning fire, charging the tongue with dryness and soot," which makes fevers so malignant.

It can be seen, then, that the phenomenology of the purity and of the impurity of fire is built up from the most elementary phenomenal forms. We have given only a few of these forms by way of example, and perhaps have already worn out the patience of our reader. But this impatience in itself is a sign; we would like the realm of values to be a closed realm. We would like to judge values without bothering about the primary empirical meanings. Now it seems clear that many values do nothing but perpetuate the privileged status of certain objective experiences, so that there results an inextricable intermixture of facts and values. It is this intermixture that a psychoanalysis of objective knowledge must sort out. When imagination has "precipitated" the unreasoned, materialistic elements, it will have more liberty for the construction of new scientific experiments.

But the true idealization of fire is arrived at by following the phenomenological dialectic of fire and light. Like all the dialectics based on perception that we find at the root of the dialectical sublimation, the idealization of fire through light rests on a phenomenal contradiction: sometimes fire shines without burning; then its value is all purity. For Rilke, "To be loved means to be consumed in the flame; to love is to shine with an inexhaustible light." For to love is to escape from doubt, it is to live in the certainty of the heart.

This transformation of fire into light through a process of idealization appears indeed to be the principle of the transcendence of Novalis, if we attempt to apprehend this principle in its closest possible relation to phenomena. According to Novalis, "Light is the essence of the igneous phenomenon." Light is not only a symbol but an agent of purity. "There where light finds nothing to do, nothing to separate, nothing to unite, it continues on. That which can neither be separated nor united is simple, pure." In infinite space light then does *nothing*. It awaits the eye. It awaits the soul. It is then the basis for spiritual illumination. Never perhaps has anyone drawn so much thought from a physical phenomenon as Novalis when he describes the transition from the inner fire to the celestial light. Beings who have lived by the first flame of terrestrial love finish in the exaltation of pure light. This way of self-purification is clearly indicated by Gaston Derycke in his article *The Romantic Experience* (*l'Expérience romantique*).[7] As a matter of fact, it is Novalis whom he cites: "Assuredly I was too dependent on this life—a powerful corrective was necessary . . . My love has been transformed into flame, and this flame is gradually consuming all that is earthly within me."

The "calorism" of Novalis, the depth of which we have already sufficiently discussed, is sublimated into an illuminated vision. It was in his case a sort of material necessity: one cannot see any other idealization possible for the love of Novalis except this illuminism. Perhaps it would be interesting to consider a more coordinated illuminism like that of Swedenborg and to ask oneself if by looking at this life in a primitive light one could not discover a more modestly terrestrial existence. Does the Swedenborgian fire leave any ashes? To resolve this question would be to develop the reciprocal of all the theses we have presented in this book. For us it has been sufficient to prove that such questions have a meaning, and that it would be interesting to match the psychological study of reverie with the objective study of the images that entrance us.

Conclusion

If the present work could be retained as a basis for a physics or a chemistry of reverie, as the outline of a method of determining the objective conditions of reverie, it should offer new instruments for an objective literary criticism in the most precise sense of the term. It should demonstrate that metaphors are not simple idealizations which take off like rockets only to display their insignificance on bursting in the sky, but that on the contrary metaphors summon one another and are more coordinated than sensations, so much so that a poetic mind is purely and simply a syntax of metaphors. Each poet should then be represented by a *diagram* which would indicate the meaning and the symmetry of his metaphorical coordinations, exactly as the diagram of a flower fixes the meaning and the symmetries of its floral action. There is no *real flower* that does not have this geometrical pattern. Similarly, there can be no poetic flowering without a certain synthesis of poetic images. One should not, however, see in this thesis a desire to limit poetic liberty, to impose a logic, or a reality (which is the same thing) on the poet's creation. It is objectively, after the event, after the full flowering, that we wish to discover the realism and the inner logic of a poetic work. At times some truly diverse images that one had considered to be quite opposed, incongruous, and non-cohesive, will come together and fuse into one charming image. The strangest mosaics of Surrealism will suddenly reveal a continuity of meaning; a shimmering will reveal a profound light; a glance that sparkles with irony has suddenly a flow of tenderness—the drop of a tear in the fire of a confession. Such is, then, the decisive action of the imagination: of a monster it makes a newborn babe!

But a *poetic diagram* is not merely a design: it must find the way to integrate the hesitations, the ambiguities which alone can liberate us from reality and permit us to dream; and it is here that the task that we have in mind takes on all its difficulty and all its value. We do not write poetry if we are confined to a single note, for the single note has no poetic property. If we are unable immediately to attain to an ordered multiplicity, we can always resort to dialectics as to a clang that will awaken our dormant resonances. As Armand Petitjean very aptly remarks, "The agitation of the dialectic of thought, whether with or without images, serves to give form to the Imagination as nothing else does." In any case, we must above all break the impulses of a reflex expression, psychoanalyze the familiar images in order to arrive at the metaphors, particularly the metaphors of metaphors. Then we will understand why Petitjean was able to write that the Imagination eludes the determinations of psychology—psychoanalysis included—and that it constitutes an autochthonous, autogenous realm. We subscribe to this view: rather than the will, rather than the *élan vital*, Imagination is the true source of psychic production. Psychically, we are created by our reverie—created and limited by our reverie—for it is the reverie which delineates the furthest limits of our mind. Imagination works at the summit of the mind like a flame, and it is to the region of the metaphor of metaphor, to the Dadaist region where the dream, as Tristan Tzara has seen, gives a new form to the experience, when reverie transforms forms that have previously been transformed, that we must look for the secret of the mutant forces. We must then find the way to set ourselves at the place at which the original impulse is directed into various channels, doubtless led astray by its own anarchical tendency, but also impelled by the desire to charm others. In order to be happy one must think of the happiness of another person. There is thus an alterity or an altruistic element in the most selfish enjoyments. The poetic diagram must break with the naive and egotistical ideal of the unity of composition and give rise to a *decomposition* of forces. This is the very problem of creative life: how to have a future while not forgetting the past? how to ensure that passion be made luminous without being cooled?

Now if the image becomes psychically active only through the metaphors which *decompose* it, if it creates a truly new psychism only by the most elaborate transformations, in the region of the metaphor of metaphor, then the enormous poetic production of fire images becomes understandable. We have indeed tried to show that fire is, among the makers of images, the one that is most dialecticized. It alone is *subject and object.* When one gets to the bottom of an animism, one always finds a calorism. What I recognize to be living—living in the immediate sense—is what I recognize as being hot. Heat is the proof *par excellence* of substantial richness and permanence: it alone gives an immediate meaning to vital intensity, to intensity of being. In comparison with the intensity of fire, how slack, inert, static and aimless seem the other intensities that we perceive. They are not embodiments of growth. They do not fulfil their promise. They do not become active in a flame and a light which symbolize transcendence.

As we have seen in our detailed examination, inner fire is dialectical in all its properties, a replica, as it were, of this fundamental dialectic of subject and object—so much so that it only has to flame up to contradict itself. As soon as a sentiment rises to the tonality of fire, as soon as it becomes exposed in its violence to the metaphysics of fire, one can be sure that it will become charged with opposites. When this occurs, the person in love wishes to be pure and ardent, unique and universal, dramatic and faithful, instantaneous and permanent. Confronted with the dreadful temptation, the Pasiphaé of Vielé-Griffin murmurs:

A hot breath inflames my cheeks, a glacial chill turns me to ice . . .

It is impossible to escape this dialectic: to be aware that one is burning is to grow cold; to feel an intensity is to diminish it; it is necessary to be an intensity without realizing it. Such is the bitter law of man's activity.

This ambiguity alone can properly account for the waverings of the passions. The result is that in the last analysis all the *complexes* attached to fire are painful complexes, complexes both conducive to the acquiring of a neurosis and to the writing of poetry, complexes that are reversible: one can find paradise in fire's movement or in its repose, in the flame or in the ashes.

> In the bright crystal of your eyes
> Show the havoc of fire, show its inspired works
> And the paradise of its ashes.
>
> Paul Eluard

To seize fire or to give oneself to fire, to annihilate or to be annihilated, to follow the Prometheus complex or the Empedocles complex, such is the psychological alternation which converts all values and which also reveals the clash of values. What better proof can there be that fire, in the very precise sense of C. G. Jung, is the point of departure "for a fertile archaic complex," and that a special psychoanalysis must destroy its painful ambiguities the better to set free the lively dialectics which bestow on reverie its true liberty and its true function as a creative mental process?

Footnotes

Introduction

1. *Etude sur l'évolution d'un problème de physique: la propagation thermique dans les solides* (Paris, 1928).

Chapter 1

1. A. Roy-Desjoncades, *Les Lois de la Nature,* applicables aux lois physiques de la Médecine, et au bien général de l'humanité, 2 vols. (Paris, 1788), II, 144.
2. Ducarla, *Du feu complet,* p. 307.

Chapter 2

1. Pierre Bertaux, *Hölderlin* (Paris, 1936), p. 171.
2. D'Annunzio, *Le Feu,* trans., p. 322.

Chapter 3

1. Auguste-Guillaume de Schlegel, *Oeuvres écrites en français* (Leipzig, 1846), I, 307-308.
2. F. Max Muller, *Origine et développement de la Religion,* trans. J. Darmesteter (1879), p. 190.
3. Bernadin de Saint-Pierre, *Etudes de la Nature* (4th ed.; 1791), IV, 34.
4. Chateaubriand, *Voyage en Amérique,* pp. 123-124.
5. J. G. Frazer, *Le Rameau d'Or,* 3 vols., trans., III, 474.
6. J. G. Frazer, *Myths of the Origin of Fire,* pp. 8-9.
7. *Ibid.,* p. 21.
8. *Ibid.,* p. 22.
9. *Ibid.,* p. 23.
10. *Ibid.,* p. 33.
11. Quoted by Albert Béguin, *L'Ame romantique et le rêve,* 2 vols. (1937), I, 191.
12. Novalis, *Henri d'Ofterdingen,* trans., p. 241, note p. 191.

13. Novalis, *loc. cit.*, p. 237.
14. *See* Charles Nodier, second preface of *Smarra.*
15. Novalis, *loc. cit.*, p. 227.

Chapter 4

1. J.-B. Robinet, *De la Nature,* 4 vols. (3rd ed.; Amsterdam, 1766), I, 217.
2. Robinet, *loc. cit.*, I, 219.
3. Robinet, *loc. cit.*, IV, 234.
4. Novalis, *Journal intime*, followed by *Maximes inédites* (Paris), p. 106.
5. De Malon, *Le conservateur du sang humain, ou la saignée demontrée toujours pernicieuse et souvent mortelle* (1767), p. 146.
6. Jean-Pierre David, *Traité de la Nutrition et de l'accroissement précédé d'une dissertation sur l'usage des eaux de l'amnios.*
7. Pierre-Jean Fabre, *L'Abrégé des secrets chimiques* (Paris, 1636), p. 374.
8. Comte de La Cépède, *Essai sur l'électricité naturelle et artificielle,* 2 vols. (Paris, 1871), II, 169.
9. *Cosmopolite ou nouvelle lumière clymique* (Paris, 1723), p. 7.
10. *La Formation de l'esprit scientifique*, Contribution à une psychanalyse de la connaissance objective (Paris, Vrin, 1938).
11. Nicolas de Locques, *Les Rudiments de la philosophie naturelle touchant le système du corps mixte*, 2 vols. (Paris, 1665).
12. Trans. note: A pelican was a type of still used by the alchemists.
13. *La Lumière sortant de soi-même des ténèbres,* written in Italian verse, trans. by B. D. L. (2nd ed.; Paris, 1693).
14. Novalis, *Henri d'Ofterdingen*, trans., p. 186.
15. Max Scheler, *Nature et forme de la sympathie*, trans., p. 120.
16. D'Annunzio, *Le Feu,* trans., p. 325.
17. Paul Valéry, *Pièces sur l'art,* p. 13.
18. Paul Valéry, *loc. cit.*, p. 9.

Chapter 5

1. Boerhaave, *Eléments de Chimie*, 2 vols., trans. (Leyde, 1752), I, 144.
2. Charles-Guillaume Scheele, *Traité chimique de l'air et du feu,* trans. (Paris, 1781).
3. R.-P. Castel, *L'Optique des couleurs* (Paris, 1740), p. 34.
4. Ducarla, *loc. cit.*, p. 4.
5. Boerhaave, *loc. cit.*, I, 145.
6. Carra, *Dissertation élémentaire sur la nature de la lumière, de la chaleur, du feu et de l'électricité* (London, 1787), p. 50.
7. Marat, *Découvertes sur le feu, l'électricité et la lumière, constatées par une suite d'expériences nouvelles* (Paris, 1779), p. 28.
8. Blaise Vigenère, *Traité du feu et du sel* (Paris, 1622), p. 60.
9. Jourdain Guibelet, *Trois Discours philosophiques* (Evreux, 1603), p. 22.
10. Boerhaave, *loc. cit.*, I, 303.
11. Robinet, *loc. cit.*, I, p. 44.
12. Joachim Poleman, *Nouvelle lumière de Médecine du mistère du soufre des philosophes,* trans. from the Latin (Rouen, 1721), p. 145.
13. Guibelet, *loc. cit.*, p. 22.
14. Abbé de Mangin, *Question nouvelle et intéressante sur l'électricité* (Paris, 1749), pp. 17, 23, 26.

15. Winckler, *Essai sur la nature, les effets et les causes de l'électricité*, trans. (Paris, 1748), p. 139.
16. Jean-Baptiste Fayol, *L'harmonie céleste* (Paris, 1672), p. 320.
17. David, *loc. cit.*, pp. 290, 292.
18. *Lettre philosophique*, sequel to the *Cosmopolite* (Paris, 1723), pp. 9, 12.
19. Reynier, *Du feu et de quelques-uns de ses principaux effets* (Lausanne, 1787), pp. 29, 34.
20. Boerhaave, *loc. cit.*, II, 876.
21. Nicolas de Locques, *Les Rudiments de la philosophie naturelle touchant le système du corps mixte* (Paris, 1665), pp. 36, 47.
22. Hecquet, *De la digestion et des maladies de l'estomac* (Paris, 1712), p. 263.
23. *Cosmopolite, loc. cit.*, p. 113.
24. *Lettre philosophique*, sequel to the *Cosmopolite, loc. cit.*, p. 18.
25. Poleman, *loc. cit.*, p. 167.
26. Nicolas de Locques, *loc. cit.*, I, 52.
27. Crosset de la Heaumerie, *Les secrets les plus cachés de la philosophie des anciens* (Paris, 1722), p. 299.
28. Reynier, *loc. cit.*, pp. 39, 43.
29. Nicolas de Locques, *loc. cit.*, p. 46.

Chapter 6

1. Quoted and commented upon by Albert Béguin, *L'Ame romantique et le* rêve, 2 vols. (Marseille, 1937), II, 62.
2. Cf. Théophile Gautier, *Les Jeunes-France, Le Bol de Punch*, p. 244.
3. Armand Petitjean, *Imagination et Réalisation* (Paris, 1936), *passim.*
4. Marie Bonaparte, *Edgar Poe* (Paris), *passim.*
5. Jallabert, *Expériences sur l'électricité avec quelques conjectures sur la cause de ses effets* (Paris, 1749), p. 293.
6. Martine, *Dissertations sur la chaleur, trans.* (Paris, 1751), p. 350.
7. Without name of author. *Chimie du Goût et de l'Odorat ou Principe pour composer facilement, et à peu de frais, les liqueurs à boire et les eaux de senteur* (Paris, 1755), p. V.
8. Balzac, *Le Cousin Pons* (ed. Calmann-Lévy), p. 172.
9. Emile Zola, *Le Docteur Pascal*, p. 227.

Chapter 7

1. Max Scheler, *Nature et Formes de la sympathie*, trans., p. 270.
2. Novalis, *Journal intime*, followed by *Fragments inédits*, trans., p. 143.
3. Virgil, *Georgics*, Book I, line 84 and foll.
4. Pierre-Jean Fabre, *loc. cit.*, p. 6.
5. De Malon, *Le Conservateur du sang humain* (Paris, 1767), p. 135.
6. De Pezanson, *Nouveau Traite des fièvres* (Paris, 1690), pp. 30, 49.
7. See *Cahiers du Sud*, May number, 1937, p. 25.

QUARTET ENCOUNTERS

The purpose of this paperback series is to bring together influential and outstanding works of twentieth-century European literature in translation. Each title has an introduction by a distinguished contemporary writer, describing a personal or cultural 'encounter' with the text, as well as placing it within its literary and historical perspective.

Quartet Encounters will concentrate on fiction, although the overall emphasis is upon works of enduring literary merit, whether biography, travel, history or politics. The series will also preserve a balance between new and older works, between new translations and reprints of notable existing translations. Quartet Encounters provides a much-needed forum for prose translation, and makes accessible to a wide readership some of the more unjustly neglected classics of modern European literature.

Hermann Broch · *The Sleepwalkers*

Translated from the German by Willa and Edwin Muir
with an introduction by Michael Tanner
'One of the greatest European novels . . .
masterful' Milan Kundera

E.M. Cioran · *The Temptation to Exist*

Translated from the French by Richard Howard
with an introduction by Susan Sontag
'Cioran is one of the most delicate minds of real power writing today. Nuance, irony, and refinement are the essence of his thinking . . .' Susan Sontag

Stig Dagerman · *The Games of Night*

Translated from the Swedish by Naomi Walford
with an introduction by Michael Meyer
'One is haunted by a secret and uneasy suspicion that [Dagerman's] private vision, like Strindberg's and Kafka's, may in fact be nearer the truth of things than those visions of the great humanists, such as Tolstoy and Balzac, which people call universal'
Michael Meyer